RESEARCHING CHILDREN'S EXPERIENCES

RESEARCHING CHILDREN'S EXPERIENCES

Melissa Freeman
Sandra Mathison

LEARNING
RESOURCES
CENTRE

THE GUILFORD PRESS
New York   London

Printed in the United States of America

This book is printed on acid-free paper.

Last digit is print number: 9   8   7   6   5   4   3   2   1

Library of Congress Cataloging-in-Publication Data

Freeman, Melissa.
     Researching children's experiences / Melissa Freeman, Sandra Mathison.
          p. cm.
     Includes bibliographical references and indexes.
     ISBN 978-1-59385-995-4 (pbk.: alk. paper) — ISBN 978-1-59385-996-1
(hardcover: alk. paper)
     1. Child psychology—Research.   2. Experience in children.
I. Mathison, Sandra.   II. Title.
     BF722.F74 2009
     155.4072—dc22

                                                                2008036612

For Genevieve and Ava
—M. F.

For Colin, my unwitting muse on childhood
—S. M.

Preface

This book is meant to describe and show how researchers can do research with children and youth from a social constructivist methodological perspective. It therefore emphasizes the theory and practice of eliciting and understanding children's lived experience, a reality of importance to children. Their everyday experiences shape their sense of self and their views of others, and each individual's knowledge claim is seen as legitimate in its own right; however, we also acknowledge the shaping effects of culture and location. We emphasize throughout the book a need to pay attention to the social setting within which research with children is done. A social constructivist analysis situates us apart from a behavioral or psychological analysis in that we seek to understand children's experiences through their words, images, and actions in their interactions with others and with us as researchers.

The book is not, however, a simple recipe for doing research with children. It provides a well-grounded epistemological rationale for doing research with children and outlines the pragmatics of negotiating and gaining access, of the ethical issues entailed in researching youth, of data-collection strategies that work well with children and youth, and of ways to approach the analysis and interpretation of data. Given contextual differences and our commitment to understanding children's experiences in ways meaningful to them and as co-constructed within the research interaction, it is difficult to prescribe how a social constructivist informed research study with children or youth will necessarily proceed. Ordinarily, a research design is the glue that makes a study coherent and purposeful. The research design suggests what kinds of questions are asked, how research participants are chosen, what data-collection methods will be used, and how and by whom the data will be analyzed. Although we do not explicitly discuss research design, the book provides researchers with guidance on all these aspects of how to do research with children: how to identify children as research participants, how to negotiate access to and develop relationships with them, and how to collect meaningful data about their experiences.

The one facet of research design we do not deal with directly is defining appropriate research questions for understanding children's experiences. However, the many examples used in the book provide the reader with a grounded sense of what an appropriate research question is when a researcher assumes that children and youth are meaning-making individuals who have genuine knowledge about their experiences, both apart from and as part of the research process. We have included examples from our own research with children alongside a growing body of research about children and youth experiences within a social constructivist perspective.

The book can, in essence, be read as three parts. Chapters 1 through 5 outline the theoretical and relational framework for a social constructivist research perspective for understanding children and youth lived experiences. This perspective includes an analysis of alternative conceptions of childhood, issues in and advice for developing relationships with children (ones that are often mediated by institutions and adults), and especially how to think about the ethicality of those relationships. The second part of the book, Chapters 6 through 9, provides detailed guidance on data collection and analysis when doing research with children. These chapters focus more on data-collection approaches that position youth as active respondents or contributors to the research (in keeping with the social constructivist perspective) and less on already well-documented approaches such as participant observation, although there are many research examples included that rely on observational techniques. Chapter 10, the third part, previews an important perspective on research with children and youth: children as research collaborators and children as researchers. This perspective is a natural extension of a social constructivist perspective, and so this chapter encompasses in some ways the next steps in an evolving sense of the efficacy of children and youth to understand and communicate the nature of their experience. For each chapter, we have included discussion questions that will help readers connect the ideas to their own research situation or extend their thinking about the ideas.

The ultimate point of the book is to encourage reflection about what it means to do research with children and youth, to raise questions about our taken-for-granted conceptions of children, research relationships (especially as mediated by cultural and institutional norms), and children's proprietary rights of knowledge for and about them. We proffer a particular perspective on these conceptions, but our hope is that our perspective challenges more than converts researchers who find children's experiences worthy of study.

Acknowledgments

Within every book lurks the influence of many. To say we could not have done it alone is obvious, and we are grateful to families, colleagues, and research participants for all they have provided and taught us.

Thanks to C. Deborah Laughton, our editor at The Guilford Press, for her enthusiasm about books, houses, and gardens, and for her support for this book.

This book is a culmination of many research efforts involving children over the years, and we are indebted to every child who thought it worthwhile to teach us something. We are especially grateful for the funding provided by the National Science Foundation for our research on children's perspectives of state-mandated testing in upstate New York. We would like to thank all those who worked with us on this research project—children, parents, teachers, administrators, research assistants, and especially Kristen Campbell Wilcox, who helped plan and conduct interviews with kids.

For helpful conversations and comments on earlier versions of the book, thanks to Jane Agee, Jodi Kaufmann, and Kathy Roulston. We also thank reviewers: Abigail M. Jewkes, Hunter College, City University of New York; M. Elizabeth Graue, University of Wisconsin; Laurie Schroeder, University of La Verne; and Sara Davis, University of Arkansas at Fort Smith. And thanks to our partners, Tom Freeman and E. Wayne Ross, without whose friendship and love we would never accomplish anything, and to our children, Genevieve, Ava, and Colin, who contribute immeasurably to what we know and, more importantly, do not know about the life of children.

Contents

CHAPTER 1

Conceptions of Children and Childhood

There is not one childhood, but many, formed at the intersection of different cultural, social and economic systems, natural and man-made physical environments. Different positions in society produce different experiences.

—FRØNES (1993, as quoted in James & Prout, 1997, p. xiii)

How we think knowledge is acquired shapes the research process from design through analysis. We adopt a social constructivist perspective in our discussion of doing research with and about children. This perspective posits that there are no naturally occurring concepts or subjects and that all knowledge and beliefs about the world are active human constructions and, as such, are mediated by the social, historical, institutional, and economic conditions within which these constructions occur. Social constructivists position research participants, whether adults or children, as active co-constructors of meaning and understanding. Conducting social constructivist research, therefore, requires an awareness of competing meanings and assumptions and a recognition that new understandings are partial, are contextually bound, and are the result of a unique set of dynamics created when particular individuals (researchers and participants) interact in particular settings.

In this chapter, we outline the dominant theoretical perspectives that influence how children as research participants and childhood in general as a social category have been constituted across disciplines. More specifically, we describe the historical and theoretical precedents to the social constructivist perspective adopted in this book and address these questions: What is childhood? What are its historical meanings? How have these perspectives on childhood shaped research with children? What is social constructivism? Why take a social constructivist perspective on children's experience? What does a social constructivist perspective suggest for designing research?

HISTORICAL PERSPECTIVES OF CHILDHOOD

Children have not always been seen as active constructors of social meaning. The shift from the commonly held view that children are developmentally immature and incomplete, and therefore unreliable respondents, to one that seeks and values their viewpoints has occurred over many decades and across many disciplines. Children, regardless of how they were perceived by society, have always existed, even when their lived experiences may not have been of interest to philosophers or social scientists. The modern view of childhood as a separate, vulnerable, and developmental stage of life emerged in Europe between the 15th and 18th centuries, along with other shifts in perspectives about family life, labor, and education (Caputo, 1995; Christensen & Prout, 2005; James, Jenks, & Prout, 1998).

During this period, various philosophies of childhood were proffered. Although the Puritans viewed children as innately evil (Kellett, Robinson, & Burr, 2004), the Age of Reason ushered in British philosopher John Locke's (1632–1704) notion that children had no innate tendencies. He portrayed children's minds as tabula rasa, or blank slates that could be shaped in different ways, thus emphasizing the importance of a good education. Swiss philosopher Jean-Jacques Rousseau (1712–1778), in turn, suggested that children were good by nature and that it was society that corrupted them, thereby advancing his theory of education as shaping and channeling children's impulses. Early in the 19th century, Friedrich Froebel (1782–1852) invented kindergarten, the first institution to capture the notion of child centeredness. Although Locke's, Rousseau's, and Froebel's views of childhood and children differed, they all saw children as fundamentally different from adults.

The rise of cultural anthropology in the 20th century offered another perspective on the cultural construction of childhood. Even when early ethnographies were not focused on children's perspectives, rich descriptions of children's activities in different cultural settings challenged the notion of a universal developmental process (James, 2001). James explains that the disciplinary agenda of what became known as "the culture and personality school of American anthropology" (p. 247) in the 1930s and 1940s, although focused on the socialization process, advanced the view of children as "competent interpreters of the social world" (p. 246). For example, Margaret Mead's work in Papua Guinea looked at the way children's activities, playmates, teachers, and parents affected their development and provided ample support for the role that context and culture played in the development of children. Gradually, the importance of closely observing children spread, and an interest in how children themselves understood and interpreted their social worlds became the departure point for socialization studies.

For example, in sociology, Denzin (1977) questioned the usual practice of asking how it is that children become adult and considered instead what can be learned about socialization and children's cultures by asking, "how it is that children do not act adultlike" (p. 58). In education, Corsaro (2003) explored how cultural learning took place in American and Italian early childhood classrooms by observing and talking to children during their everyday classroom activities. Later he concluded, "Children do not simply imitate or internalize the world around them. They strive to interpret or make sense of their culture and to participate in it. In attempting to make sense of the adult world, children come to collectively produce their own peer worlds and cultures" (Cosaro, 2005, p. 24), a view consistent with social constructivism.

Other historical events have added to these shifting views of childhood. The 1989 United Nations Convention on the Rights of the Child has played a role not only in recognizing the rights of children (Davis, 1998) but in valuing and taking seriously children's subjective perspectives (Hogan, 2005). For example,

> Article 12 states that children not only have a right to articulate their opinions with regard to issues that affect them but have a right to have

these opinions heard. . . . Article 13 declares the child had a right to seek, receive and impart information and ideas of all kinds and Article 29 indicates that children's education should respect the child's cultural identity, language and values. (Davis, 1998, p. 325)

By focusing on how children and youth construct meaning, social scientists began to acknowledge children's active role in society, as cocreators of that society, not just absorbers of it. From a social constructivist perspective, the actions and interactions of children play a key role in shaping the environment, which, in turn, shapes them. To study children as only recipients of information within environments misses this important interaction. Not only does environment play a role in shaping how children behave, think, act, and talk, but how they do these things, in turn, shapes the environment. As we show in later chapters, different data-collection methods emphasize different parts of this relationship, some emphasizing children's perceptions of their world, others observing the interactions themselves.

THEORIES OF SOCIALIZATION

A social constructivist perspective assumes that humans, children and adults, play an active role in their own socialization process. The effects of context or the personal attributes of an agent such as age, gender, or race are not minimized; they are understood to be interactive, complex, dynamic, and ever changing. P. A. Adler and Adler (1998) identify three common socialization models of childhood: developmental, normative socialization, and social constructionist. Each perspective places different emphases on the role that biology and environment play and present differing viewpoints on the contributions an individual child's perspective is seen to make.

Developmental Model

Developmental models of socialization regard childhood as a developmental period in which children progress through established cognitive and biological stages. In this perspective, children are in the process of "becoming" someone other, not as "being" someone themselves (Morss, 1996). They are viewed as incomplete, immature, and irrational beings who acquire maturity and rationality over time.

> Central to this mode of thought are three elements: "naturalness," "universality," and "rationality" . . . the child is seen as progressing from simplicity to complexity, from irrational to rational behavior, from a stage of biological immaturity, passing through a developmental process and moving into fully developed human status as adults. (Christensen & Prout, 2005, p. 48)

At the root of developmental theories is Darwinian evolutionism. G. Stanley Hall, a founder of child study in the United States, was deeply committed to the idea that childhood followed a natural, evolutionary course of progress.

In this view, studies involving children might document age-related competencies (Hogan, 2005) or study the impact of specific socialization variables for what they reveal about adult personality characteristics (Qvortrup, 1990). Children are portrayed as outcomes of socialization or as variables within a socialization process (James & Prout, 1997). Even though there are no consistent findings connecting a child's upbringing with a particular adult personality, "studies still continued to inscribe themselves in this tradition, suggesting the persuasive power of the idea of a cultural connection between the socialization of the small child and adult life" (Christensen & Prout, 2005, p. 47).

On the one hand, this view has supported the belief that children are not worthy of study in their own right because they are not fully formed individuals, and their lack of maturity and rationality makes them unreliable as informants (Hogan, 2005). Under this model, adults, such as parents, teachers, or psychologists, are consulted if the need to understand a child arises. On the other hand, studies focusing on developmental processes have contributed to the advancement of constructivist perspectives by showing that a natural course of maturation does not happen in isolation, suggesting the need for more interactive models, including both biology and the environment. John Dewey (1859–1952) and Jean Piaget (1896–1980), although emphasizing different aspects of cognition and learning, both agreed that, for the best possible results in social, emotional, and cognitive growth, the environment, learning condition, or task needs to be appropriately matched to and respect children's natural characteristics and developmental stages. The idea of an environment–maturation correspondence led to theories of readiness on the one hand and to interactive theories, such as social constructivism, on the other. The focus of many developmental studies, however, remains that of demonstrating universal processes, not of exploring an individual's understanding of these processes.

Normative Socialization Model

Normative socialization models are built on Locke's belief that children come to the world as blank slates. These perspectives, of which behaviorism and social learning theories are prime examples, have focused on the ways social norms are internalized by children and the role stimuli play in that process. Behaviorism has had a very significant impact on childhood studies, taking hold in American psychology with the work of John B. Watson (1878–1958), who responded to the logical positivist call for scientific, empirical, and objective research. Watson proffered that children learn society's desirable behaviors through positive and negative stimuli and learn to respond and behave appropriately once they internalized the desired behavior. The child is seen as a passive recipient who learns by internalizing the surrounding adult culture. B. F. Skinner (1904–1990) suggested, however, that humans do not merely respond to external stimuli but act on their environment to produce certain effects. The consequences of those actions are also internalized along with the corresponding responses suggesting that people take a more active role in their own socialization. Here again, however, the focus is on developing universal theories used to influence the behaviors of children, not on understanding the children themselves.

Social Constructionist Perspective

The social constructionist view is an interactionist perspective built on the belief that children are social actors and that socialization is an interactive, social process whereby children simultaneously act on their environment while also being shaped by it. Because children are believed to take an active role in their own learning by interpreting the world around them, understanding socialization has necessitated new methods, ones that seek out and, in many cases, prioritize children's perspectives. This focus on the individual-in-context has meant that childhood can no longer be understood without some consideration for history, society, and culture, and thus any universal notions of childhood can only be seen as flawed. This perspective has played a prominent role in the development of constructivist frameworks for theories of learning, cognition, and pedagogy and for the development of theoretical frameworks guiding research such as social constructivism and the new social studies of childhood. A more detailed distinction between constructionism and constructivism as theoretical frameworks for research is made later in this chapter.

NEW SOCIAL STUDIES OF CHILDHOOD

The advancement of a constructionist view on childhood is made clear in the proliferation of a child-centered perspective that James et al. (1998) call the "new social studies of childhood." Although not always recognized as the dominant view, it is characterized as an interdisciplinary movement that has emerged simultaneously from sociology, social anthropology, developmental psychology, social geography, education, and social work. Principles of the new social studies of childhood are as follows:

- Childhood is a distinct and intrinsically interesting and important phase in human experience, valued for its own unique qualities rather than for its resemblance to adulthood.
- Children are viewed, therefore, as fully formed and complete individuals with a perspective of their own rather than as partially developed, incompletely formed adults.
- Children are autonomous subjects rather than members (or even possessions) of their family; their parents' and family members' interests and views are no longer assumed to be identical to their own.
- Children have rights of their own, including the right to protection from harm and the right to voice opinions and influence decisions in matters relating to their own lives. (Brooker, 2001, pp. 162–163)

As we show in the next section, these principles do not necessarily translate into a single approach for researching children. They

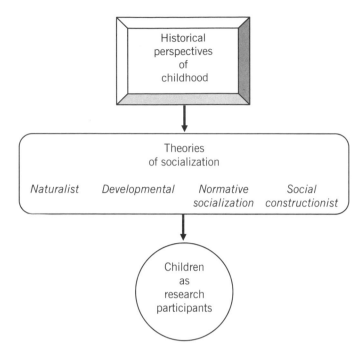

FIGURE 1.1. Constituting factors in studies of childhood.

do, however, alter the roles that children and their experiences are given in research designs.

Figure 1.1 illustrates how multiple theoretical perspectives have shaped the conception of research with children.

Children as Research Participants

It seems quite natural that children would be running around playing games in a playground or required to learn to read and write at school. It also seems natural that children are not expected to know as much or to be able to do as much as adults. It is not obvious to think of these things as constructed by human society and culture and not a natural part of childhood. The view that childhood is a temporary stage progressing toward, and different from, adulthood still shapes how social institutions such as the family and school are organized (e.g., age-based classrooms, parental permission before access or treatment, child protection laws, age-based laws prohibiting access to certain substances such as alcohol) and infiltrate how we think about and work with children, even when working from other perspectives.

James et al. (1998, p. 4) describe four conceptions of children that recast them as active and meaningful participants in social life: the socially constructed child, the tribal child, the social structural child, and the minority group child.

The socially constructed child questions the biological determinism of the developing child approach and views children and childhoods as varied across settings, time, and cultures. For example, whereas a 7-year-old may be seen as needing supervision in one household, in another household that 7-year-old may be expected to watch a 3-year-old sibling while the parent runs errands. Such views are not just variations in parenting styles but are often evidence of different cultural beliefs about children's competencies and their role in the family and society. Although children may be biologically immature, this immaturity is understood differently, a meaning that is cultural.

In this conception, children's experiences become meaningful in relation to multiple contexts, and this dynamic needs to be taken into account in analysis. Children and adults are part of a culture they reproduce, interpret, and reinterpret, often in interactions with one another and with peer groups. Individual development thus becomes embedded in children's collective weaving of their places in the webs of significance that constitute their culture. The social study of children and childhood must, therefore, acknowledge the interplay between adults' and children's perspectives on social relations and cultures (Christensen & Prout, 2005, p. 50). Young people's perspectives are interpreted in specific cultural contexts, for example, to examine how identities are formed through social identification and academic learning in a ninth-grade classroom (Wortham, 2006) or to understand the positive educational development of black middle-school girls in an urban setting (Evans-Winters, 2005).

The tribal child is the "empirical" and "politicized" version of the socially constructed child. In this perspective, children are viewed as constructing autonomous, separate worlds from adults: childhood as a sort of exotic tribe with its own beliefs and practices. The tribal worlds children create independently from adult worlds are the focus. The research emphasis is giving voice to children and redressing the silencing they experience through adult-centered research agendas. For example, anthropologist Charlotte Hardman questioned the practice of studying children as future beings and suggested that children should be studied for what they had to say about their own present world, as people in their own right (Caputo, 1995). Hardman's (1973) study of children's games, beliefs, and relations in a school playground in Oxford, England, and Opie and Opie's (1959/2000) study of children's songs, rules, and rituals illustrate understanding how children's activities construct a social world that is different from adults' constructions of the world.

Researchers working from the tribal child perspective often use ethnographic methods such as participant observation for understanding children's cultures. This allows researchers to observe children's actions and interactions without imposing an adult perspective. A criticism of this approach is that it often omits the daily interactions children do have with adults that invariably impinge on children's conceptions of their world (Alanen & Mayall, 2001; Mayall, 1996; Punch, 2003). Many social constructivists argue that these are not separate worlds that are being constructed but rather different perspectives made out of the symbols, images, structures, and other meaning systems and discourses shared by children and adults alike. This understanding has resulted in social constructivist studies that focus solely on children's social worlds within specific social or institutional settings, such as the way 9- to 11-year-old girls construct social order through talk and games (Goodwin, 2006).

The social structural child perspective understands childhood as a universal category, a socially structured position present in all societies. The focus is on how macrostructures, such as age, gender, race, class, religion, or disability, interact with other social categories such as culture, location, and the economy (e.g., Nieuwenhuys, 1994; Reynolds, 1991). Researchers working from this perspective focus on what studies of children's cultures reveal about predetermined categories used in their research. For example, in a study on street children in Paraguay, Glauser (1990) illustrated how the category "street children" is used to identify a social group, but differences in the daily lives of street children inevitably force a reconceptualization of the construct itself. Social structural studies seek to bring new understandings to complex topics, such as school achievement, by eliciting and comparing the lived experiences of African American and Latino youth living in two distinct neighborhoods (Carter, 2005). In that way, the macrostructures of race and gender are given new meaning through the eyes of the youth living within them.

The minority group child is the politicized version of the social structural child and emphasizes the minority, and thus oppressed status of children in society and, in turn, highlights their civil rights. Researchers within this perspective do not necessarily view children as different or less capable than adults, but they do view them "as a minority group who lack power to influence the quality of their lives" (Mayall, Bendelow, Storey, & Veltman, 1996, p. 207). Research from this perspective focuses on children's views of an adult world they are powerless to shape and their experiences in institutions in which they are required to participate. The focus is on children's perceptions of the adult world, especially in areas where children's participation or experience is similar, such as children's views of social services, health issues, or work in which both adults and children participate and yet differ on account of their social status as children and their increased vulnerability to exploitation (Punch, 2003). For example, Qvortrup (1994) suggests children can be characterized as a minority group in relation to adults because this relationship is characterized by marginalization, paternalism, protection, and institutionalization.

> The crucial distinction that makes children children is that they are not adults; as individuals and as a social group, they lack adulthood. This lack can be defined variously as deficiency, disadvantage, and/ or oppression. The components may vary according to individual and societal standpoint. What is common to the intergenerational relationship of children to adults is that children are inferior to adults. This inferiority is demonstrated in many ways: Children are not allowed to make decisions affecting them; must defer to adult knowledge and authority; have little economic power. More generally, one may say that, in any given society, the relationships between generations are governed by generational contracts, which set out adults' understandings of the division of labor in that society, and the permitted and required activities of children. The inferiority of children is demonstrated, if we needed further demonstration, by the fact that they have little negotiating power as regards the intergenerational contract. They must work within it. (Mayall, 1994, pp. 118–119)

These four sociological perspectives are not static and separate categories, but each emphasizes particular social constructs over others. In reality, studies of children and childhood often transcend one perspective to include other perspectives as well. For example,

Punch's (2003) study of the nature of children's work and play in rural Bolivia took a tribal and a minority child view, emphasizing both the cultural world created by children interacting with children but seeking also to understand how children's work and play are situated within Bolivian culture. Similarly, Holloway and Valentine's (2000) research on globalization and children's use of the Internet seeks to combine all four perspectives.

These four perspectives, although different from each other, can be further differentiated from the developing child perspective, that is, how well their behaviors confirm or disconfirm preexisting developmental theories. What these perspectives have in common is that childhood is no longer taken for granted as being one thing. There is a growing understanding of how different assumptions about children affect the topics studied, study designs, the researcher–participant relationship, and the way in which children and adults are represented in research reports.

Constructivism and Constructionism

The terms "constructivism" and "constructionism" are closely related and sometimes used interchangeably. They both emphasize the socially constructed nature of knowledge and reality, that is, "the view that all knowledge, and therefore all meaningful reality as such, is contingent upon human practices, being constructed in and out of interaction between human beings and their world, and developed and transmitted within an essentially social context" (Crotty, 1998, p. 42). However, the terms emphasize different aspects of this relationship. The use of constructivism has roots in rational philosophy and developmental psychology and focuses on the individual's active engagement with his or her environment.

> Constructivists propose that each individual mentally constructs the world of experience. In this sense, the mind is not a mirror of the world as it is, but functions to create the world as we know it. From this perspective there could be as many realities as there are minds to conceptualize or construe. (Gergen, 1999, p. 236)

For constructivists, meaning gets constructed in the individual mind, whereas "social" constructionists argue there is no such thing as an individual or separate mind, since all humans live in a social world that is constituted by language, rules, norms, and social relationships. Social constructionism, having roots in interpretive sociology, emphasizes the social construction of meaning and the power of language and discourse in shaping that meaning.

> Constructivisim . . . points out the unique experience of each of us. It suggests that each one's way of making sense of the world is as valid and worthy of respect as any other, thereby tending to scotch any hint of a critical spirit. On the other hand, social constructionism emphasizes the hold our culture has on us: It shapes the way in which we see things (even in the way in which we feel things!) and gives us a quite definite view of the world. (Crotty, 1998, p. 58)

Research on childhood and children has been influenced by both social constructionism and constructivism. James and Prout (1990) have done much to advance a social constructionist view of childhood that posits childhood as a discursive formation within which different children and childhoods are formed and constituted. Developmental psychologist Lev Vygotsky's (1896–1934) belief that individual learning is the result of one's engagement in a social and cultural world has done much to advance the importance of context in constructivist theories. As epistemologies, both theories emphasize the constructed nature of reality as individuals engage with the social world, creating an overlap between constructivism and social constructionism, which has resulted in a third term: "social constructivism."

> In this case, it is proposed that individuals mentally construct the world, but they do so largely with categories supplied by social relationships. For the social constructivist therapist, for example, there may be an intense interest in the narratives an individual brings into therapy, but these narratives are treated as psychological. The therapist might thus explore what they mean to the person, and how central they are to his or her ways of thinking. In effect, we have a new position that borrows from both traditions, and thereby opens a new range of possibilities. (Gergen, 1999, p. 237)

Researchers working within a social constructivist perspective assume that individuals are always interacting with a socially constituted environment and that these interactions form the basis of their experiences. A social constructivist approach breaks from the common assumption that children experience life in a universal manner across time and place. This book takes a social constructivist approach to researching children's lived experience to emphasize the lived experiences of children and the constructed nature of research. Although children's experiences may be only one perspective among others (e.g., those of teachers and parents in a school ethnography), this book focuses on the theory and practice of eliciting and integrating children's perspectives within a social constructivist epistemology. The reality we attempt to understand through our work is a reality of importance to children. Their everyday experiences shape their sense of self and their views of others. Each individual's knowledge claim is seen as legitimate in its own right while also acknowledging the shaping effects of culture and location. Further, we emphasize throughout the book a need to pay attention to the social setting that we construct as we go about doing research with children. A social constructivist analysis situates us apart from a behaviorist or psychological analysis in that we seek to understand children's experiences through the words, images, and actions children convey in their interactions with others and us as researchers. Although the analytic emphasis might shift from focusing solely on children's interactions as in a tribal child approach to one that

---

1. REALITIES are constructed as and from experience.
2. TRUTHS are relative to the context of observation.
3. KNOWLEDGE is constructed from social and individual assumptions and developed through language.
4. MEANING is constructed both internally and socially through interpretation.
5. KNOWING is an ongoing process of interpreting present events from within the observer's interpretive framework.
6. SCIENCE is an interpretive process by which observers test consensually derived distinctions for their utility.
7. Each element in a social system is RECURSIVE and provides conditions of operation for other elements in the social system.
8. PERSONS have agency and choice, although they are constrained by recursive interactions between self and the environment.

FIGURE 1.2. Characteristics of a social constructivist epistemology. Based on Fisher (1991, p. 15).

emphasizes the shaping power of the economy or institution as in a social structural child perspective, what these perspectives have in common is the central role young people's lived experiences play in the analytic process. Figure 1.2 summarizes the characteristics of a social constructivist perspective.

Experience

Throughout this book, we advance theoretical underpinnings and methodological strategies for researching children's experiences. But what is experience? A typical dictionary definition might read: "the apprehension of an object, thought, or emotion through the sense or mind" or "an event one has participated in." Researchers interested in human experience have tried to differentiate experience from other forms of sensory or organic interactions with the world. For example, lived experience may be defined as experience prior to the mind giving it an interpreted meaning (Van Manen, 1990).

On the other hand, Dewey differentiated transactions people had with their environment that are purely physical or chemical from those that are imbued with meaning, and thus "instruments of expression and communication" (Dewey, 1934/1980, p. 25). In Dewey's conceptualization, experience is both intentional and responsive. Even a small child whose gaze is caught by a crawling ant is not simply responding to the movement of the ant but is also projecting interest or curiosity, an attitude supported by the many "Look at this!" statements expressed in interaction with others. Furthermore, the experience of seeing the ant is not just internal but is composed of the sensation of being indoors or out and other contextual layers such as whether the child was alone or with others, had time to explore, or was being tugged down the sidewalk. In Dewey's view, people participate in the world in ways that are based on previous experience, and this shapes how they respond to the new experience at hand. Learning, therefore, involves not just discovering things but a process of meaningful organization or explanation of new experiences based on one's previous experiences and on the specific features of the new interaction (Wheatley, 1991). "Experience is the result, the sign, and the reward of that interaction of organism and environment which, when it is carried to the full, is a transformation of interaction into participation and communication" (Dewey, 1934/1980, p. 22).

Investigations of experience necessitate an understanding of what is meant by experience, because what is meant by experience will determine the extent or limitation of one's access to another person's experience and how one goes about eliciting that experience. Understanding children's experience is problematic, however, because we make the assumption that we can learn about children's experience by investigating their various engagements in both social and physical worlds and by soliciting their reports of their subjective worlds. This sort of research effort is one that requires high levels of inference along the way (Greene & Hill, 2005).

Adopting a social constructivist perspective on research with children does not automatically mean rejecting the developmental, sociological, or psychological theories about children. Rather, as we discuss further in Chapter 4, it asks us to consider the way in which these theories shape our beliefs, practices, and interpretations about children as we engage with them. This orientation sees the world as dynamic, interactional, constructed, and reconstructed; therefore, our understandings of it cannot be fixed or predetermined. As we assist children in their constructions of meaning in our interactions together, our own assumptions, which have served to shape the nature of these interactions, may be challenged and reshaped. As we learn about others, we learn about ourselves; these are not separate events. According to constructivism, coming to know is always a process of reconstruction and reorganization based on experience and is constantly modified by a learner's experience of the world. Experience is never related in any pure form but is always related within a context that functions to modify the experience to fit that context. People, therefore, construct reality from experience and in experience.

Thus, researching children's experiences from a social constructivist perspective must pose questions that connect with children's lived experiences either because they are of interest to children or because they are in a unique position in relation to the topic to provide insight on it. Researchers choose research problems based on what is intellectually interesting, what has policy implications, and what is perceived to be helpful in improving the quality of life for children. If, however, one assumes that children make meaning and have experiences on their own terms apart from adult interpretations and conceptions, then researchers must also give serious consideration to issues that matter to children. Research studies that reflect what matters to children should be asking children questions like "What do you care about?," "What do you believe?," "Where do you belong?," "When do you feel strong?," "When do you feel empty?" Studies that seek children's perspectives on topics that affect their lives should be asking children questions like "How has school testing altered your experience in school?," "What do you think about the after-school offerings at the community center?"

As we demonstrate throughout the book, children's experiences have been the subject of study across the disciplines and on a variety of topics: for example, children's health in school (Mayall et al., 1996), their play (Gaunt, 2006; Goodwin, 2006; Thorne, 1993), their experience in hospitals (Alderson, 1993), their experience of living with asthma (M. Morgan, Gibbs, Maxwell, & Britten, 2002), their views of fashion (Pole, 2007), and their views on school (Carter, 2005; Dockett & Perry, 2003; Rymes, 2001). This work has contributed to a wide cross-disciplinary range of methodological resources for conducting research with children. The personal interests and biography of the researcher, the research question, and the study's purpose will affect how the perspectives of children and young people get incorporated into the research design. There is not one approach. There are, however, practices that contribute to more positive outcomes for both researchers and participants. Although a step-by-step approach to research design is anathema to a social constructivist framework, the examples and suggestions we bring together and build on regarding institutional review board (IRB) applications, gatekeepers and access, permission and consent, data collection, and data analysis offer a wide variety of design strategies and issues for the novice or experienced researcher to draw and learn from.

DISCUSSION QUESTIONS

1. Describe how your assumptions about children and childhood either align or do not align with a social constructivist perspective. Which historical assumptions, such as developmentalism, are the most difficult for you to see differently? How have you modified your conceptions based on your reading of this chapter?

2. Identify three institutional practices that are based on socially constructed notions of the positions children have in society that will

most likely affect how your study gets designed. Reflect on how these practices might constrain and support the research you hope to do with child participants. Consider how your study supports or alters these norms.

3. Select a key journal in your field. Examine the contents of the journal, looking specifically for articles in which children are the participants. Do this for the past 3 years and then also for 3 consecutive years a decade ago. How prevalent were studies involving children over these two periods? What were the primary methods used in the studies that did involve children? What were the modes of discourse used to describe children or childhood? How have things changed or stayed the same in research with children over the past couple of decades?

CHAPTER 2

Negotiating Access
for Research with Children

> Vulnerable populations include members of society who
> through economic, social, biological, or legal status may
> be more susceptible to inherent research pressures and
> thus may require special protection from research risks.
> —WAGENER ET AL. (2004, p. 336)

As views of childhood and children have changed, so have the kinds of relationships researchers seek to develop with their participants. At the same time, IRBs responsible for regulating research involving human subjects or participants, while expanding the range of studies requiring IRB approval, have not necessarily included new research methodologies. Understanding the role IRBs have played over time is key to planning and doing research with all human participants, but especially with children, considered "persons with diminished autonomy" and, therefore, "entitled to protection" (Belmont Report, 1979). This chapter provides the historical context for this regulation, addresses the tension created between a social constructivist view of children as active, knowing participants and their status as a vulnerable population, and provides practical guidelines for negotiating with IRBs for permission to do research with children.

THE REGULATION OF RESEARCH IN THE SOCIAL SCIENCES

The regulation of social science research to protect people's dignity and rights is a fairly recent event. (Often the term "human subjects" is used, although within a social constructivist perspective such a term misrepresents the nature of human involvement in research.) An ethical concern for the just treatment of people as patients can be traced back to the Greek physician Hippocrates (460–380 B.C.), who is said to have developed the Hippocratic Oath. However, international attention to the oath's mantra of "Do no harm" came to the forefront after World War II during Case 1 of the Nuremburg trials, known as the Doctors' Trial. Twenty-three doctors and administrators were found guilty of committing war crimes and crimes against humanity involving medical experiments on the effects of freezing, malaria, poisons, and bone transplantation; the euthanasia of sick and disabled civilians; the killing of Jews for anatomical research; and more. The Nuremberg Military Tribunal's judgment of August 19, 1947, included a 10-point statement delineating permissible medical experiments on human subjects, which became known as the Nuremberg code. Basic principles from that code have not changed much. Take, for example, code 1:

> The voluntary consent of the human subject is absolutely essential. This means that the person involved should have legal capacity to give consent . . . without the intervention of any element of force, fraud, deceit . . . and should have sufficient knowledge and comprehension of the elements of the subject matter involved as to enable him to make an understanding and enlightened decision. This latter element requires that before the acceptance of an affirmative decision by the experimental subject there should be made known to him the nature, duration, and purpose of the experiment; the method and means by which it is to be conducted; all inconveniences and hazards reasonable to be expected; and the effects upon his health or person which may possibly come from his participation in the experiment. (Nuremberg Military Tribunals, 1949, pp. 181–182)

This code was followed by other guidelines developed by the World Medical Assembly, starting with the *Declaration of Helsinki* in 1964 with later revisions in the 1970s and then finally in 1989. In the United States, creating guidelines for the protection of human subjects gained momentum when it became public knowledge that the Tuskegee Syphilis Study, a 30-year government-sponsored research project, had left 300 black men untreated even when treatment for syphilis was available (J. H. Jones, 1993). This led to the establishment of the National Commission for the Protection of Human Subjects of Biomedical and Behavioral Research. The recommendations from this group were published in 1979 as the Belmont Report, which serves as the basis for the current Code of Federal Regulations Title 45-Part 46 Protection of Human Subjects (45 CFR 46). In 1991, the U.S. Department of Health and Human Services issued revised regulations that are referred to as the Common Rule, which are endorsed by most federal agencies and which are applicable when federal funding for research is involved. Most organizations simply adopt the Common Rule, whether federal funding is involved or not. A key feature of these regulations is that organizations must establish an IRB that will judge proposed research based on the core principles described in the Belmont Report. IRBs, also called ethics committees or ethics review boards, consist of individuals within an organization designated to review and approve research proposals involving people.

The core principles of the Belmont Report are respect for persons, beneficence, and justice.

> Respect for persons incorporates at least two ethical convictions: first, that individuals should be treated as autonomous agents, and second, that persons with diminished autonomy are entitled to protection.

> The term "beneficence" is often understood to cover acts of kindness or charity that go beyond strict obligation. In this document, beneficence is understood in a stronger sense, as an obligation. Two general rules have been formulated . . . (1) do no harm and (2) maximize possible benefits and minimize possible harms.

> Justice [is] in the sense of "fairness in distribution" or "what is deserved." (Belmont Report, 1979)

These principles are the basis for the requirements of IRBs, including a clear process for securing informed consent from participants, an assessment of the risks and benefits to participants, and a description of participant recruitment and selection strategies.

Critiques of Governmental Regulation of Social Science Research

With governmental regulations developed to address what have been ethically and morally outrageous research practices, it seems as though such regulation would be beneficial and welcomed by researchers and participants alike. There are, however, a number of critiques of the current reach of the regulation of research and the desire for extending that reach even further.

The Common Rule applies specifically to federally funded research, but most organizations have extended the rules to all research, regardless of source of funding. Why this is the case is not entirely clear; a felt organizational responsibility for the ethical treatment of others is surely part of this, but so too is a desire to avoid litigation should harm befall a research participant.

One reason this extension is problematic is that there has been no consideration of the relevance of the rules in relation to specific research contexts or purposes of research. The application of rules meant to oversee clinical and biomedical research to all types of research has not been well received by faculty and students in disciplines such as journalism, communication studies, history, and anthropology, to name a few. Excesses in medical research sparked the development of regulations in part because patients who participated in clinical trials were often in vulnerable positions (hospitalized, incarcerated, indigent) and unable to speak for themselves. Most social science research is, however, done with children and adults who are in possession of their full faculties and able to act in their own interests. Admittedly, social science research may create uneasiness, embarrassment, or discomfort, but these are often within the scope of what the Common Rule describes as "ordinarily encountered in daily life."

At the heart of the criticism is a lack of discussion about what constitutes ethical research relationships and practices and the adoption of review procedures and practices that represents a narrow, singular conception of research. For example, key concepts such as who is a researcher, what is research, and what is meant by risk, harm, benefit, or consent are adopted by IRBs and applied across project proposals regardless of the proposals' definitions of such concepts (see Haggerty, 2004, for an example of this process). IRB procedures, and now certifications that researchers must have before submitting a research proposal for IRB approval, assume that all research is conducted as if it were clinical research. There are many ways this creates conflict for social scientists: with regard to issues of preordinate designs, fully developed data-collection protocols, and the assumption that anonymity and confidentiality are necessary. For example, historians are puzzled by demands to maintain anonymity in their data collection and reporting, a practice that runs counter to the discipline's basic strategies for judging the adequacy of historical research. Other researchers have challenged the necessity for anonymity and confidentiality, raising questions about the purpose and meaningfulness of research that is disconnected from real contexts and real people (Nespor, 2000). Indeed, there is little research that supports the assumptions that being named (either individuals or places) is harmful and that forms of anonymization are actually effective (often people and places are given pseudonyms but are still identifiable). Similarly, ethnographers are puzzled by demands to submit complete interview or observation protocols before spending any time in the field, a standard expectation for ensuring that data collection evolves in an empirically grounded way. Research being conducted with indigenous populations who have their own code of ethics (Smith, 2005), action, and participatory research (Lincoln, 2005) and research conducted with certain groups, such as queer youth (Gray, 2004), are examples of studies that find themselves at odds, for different reasons, with IRBs.

> Ethics is about supporting values such as respecting people and their communities and benefiting individuals and society. In this context, this includes doing valid research, respecting research participants and their communities in all the ways that pertain to the particular context, creating socially beneficial policies, and effectively disseminating and applying findings. However, there is no simple rule or ethical principle that produces ethical [research]. Each situation is different. (Sieber, 2004, p. 402)

NAVIGATING IRBs

The Common Rule, which was aimed at supervising federally funded research, is, for the most part, being applied by IRBs to all research involving human participants. Most research universities, medical facilities, private research facilities, and school districts have IRBs, and researchers affiliated with these organizations or who wish to conduct research with people in these organizations must submit an IRB application before beginning the study. In some instances, the approval of more than one IRB is required; for example, a university-based researcher doing research in a hospital will likely require the approval of both the university and the hospital. Before beginning a study, you will need to ask yourself: Is what I am proposing research? Since children are the targeted population, does what I propose take into account their status? Do I understand the potential risks and benefits to my participants? Do I have a process for selection and recruitment? What about for informed consent and, if required, parental permission?

Children: A Vulnerable Population

IRB guidelines define children as a vulnerable population because they are considered persons "with diminished autonomy." Inherent in this view are prevalent beliefs about children's limited capacity to understand consent-related information. Federal regulations state that additional safeguards to protect subjects' rights and welfare must be included when "some or all of the subjects are likely to be vulnerable to coercion or undue influence." Additional safeguards typically include seeking parental permission and assent from child participants.

Children are vulnerable in three ways. First, they are inherently vulnerable because of their smaller size, weaker physicality, and more limited knowledge and experience of the work of researchers. Their protection from unsafe or manipulative adults is, therefore, essential. Second, they are structurally vulnerable because they lack political, social, and economic power. This puts them in a position (described in more detail in Chapter 3) of being directly inaccessible to researchers, thus placing the decision about participation in adult hands and further diminishing children's autonomy. Finally, children are vulnerable because normative beliefs about their capacities and a reliance on developmental theories as the primary means for assessing those capacities still place age as the primary determiner of a child's rights. "There is a tendency to rely too heavily on a presumption of children's biological and psychological vulnerability in developing our law, policy and practice, and insufficient focus on the extent to which their lack of civil status creates that vulnerability" (Lansdown, 1994, p. 35).

Balancing the protection of children with their rights as citizens, therefore, is complicated. One place to begin is to seek ways to include them at every stage of research design. Understanding the way children and adolescents are socially and contextually positioned plays a crucial role in determining how to (a) assess risks and benefits, (b) develop a clear and defensible process for selection, and (c) secure informed consent. As we discuss further in Chapter 3, before gaining assent from children, one must gain *access* to children, and that often involves negotiating with multiple gatekeepers. Here we consider some of the steps to consider in planning a youth-centered study.

Assessing Risks and Benefits to Participants

"The term 'risk' refers to a possibility that harm may occur. However, when expressions such as 'small risk' or 'high risk' are used, they usually refer (often ambiguously) both to the chance (probability) of experiencing a harm and the severity (magnitude) of the envisioned harm" (Belmont Report, 1979). For example, in a study of sexually abused children's and young people's experience of the investigative interview process, there was a high probability of some emotional distress when participants recount the details of the abuse in the interview, but the magnitude of that distress would be difficult to predict ahead of time (Westcott & Davies, 1996). One indication of the stressfulness or sensitivity of a topic might be the response to recruitment efforts, but other contextual factors such as the clarity of what the study entails and the time frame for the study can also play a role, making assessment of risk all the more difficult.

One way IRBs assess whether some risk is appropriate is by weighing potential benefits against probable risks, and sometimes different levels of consent accompany different levels of risk, as illustrated in Figure 2.1. "The term 'benefit' is used in the research context to refer to something of positive value related to health or welfare" (Belmont Report, 1979). There are many kinds of risks and benefits, including psychological, physical, legal, social, and economic, and these refer not only to the individual participating in a study but also

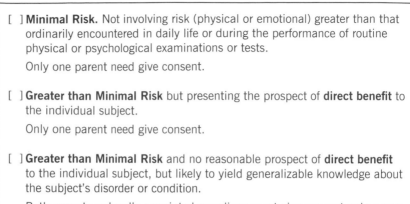

[ ] **Minimal Risk.** Not involving risk (physical or emotional) greater than that ordinarily encountered in daily life or during the performance of routine physical or psychological examinations or tests.

Only one parent need give consent.

[ ] **Greater than Minimal Risk** but presenting the prospect of **direct benefit** to the individual subject.

Only one parent need give consent.

[ ] **Greater than Minimal Risk** and no reasonable prospect of **direct benefit** to the individual subject, but likely to yield generalizable knowledge about the subject's disorder or condition.

Both parents or legally appointed guardians must give consent unless one parent or guardian is deceased, unknown, incompetent, or not reasonably available or does not have legal responsibility for the custody of the minor.

FIGURE 2.1. Sample categories for describing kinds and magnitudes of risk to child research participants.

participants' families, larger communities, and society. In the prior example, the benefit to participants who were given the opportunity to voice their satisfaction or concern about the investigative interview experience may have been outweighed by the probable distress experienced in reflecting on the experience.

An example of a different kind of risk is provided in Hessler et al.'s (2003) study of high school students' perceptions of risk. The topic was not the issue for the IRB, but the data-collection method was. The authors, employees of the Missouri Department of Health, were interested in recruiting high school students who would maintain a daily e-mail journal of their activities. The IRB's concern was that the risks associated with the disclosure of individuals' private thoughts was considerable. Concerns ranged from the lack of privacy inherent in e-mail servers, the perception of anonymity that e-mail diaries give the participants, and the ability of the research team to be able to match consent forms, and therefore individuals, with the content of their e-mails. These issues taken together prompted the researchers to work out a different recruitment process and mode of data management. Field coordinators, usually high school teachers or counselors, managed the recruitment process, consent and assent procedures, and payments to participants. The student participants created an e-mail account using a pseudonym and only used their pseudonym throughout the study. In this way, the research team would not know who was participating or be able to match individual students to their responses, but if an issue arose, such as a student reporting a situation in which he or she was being harmed or wished to harm another, the field coordinator could be notified and then work with that student. The risks to participants were thus minimized by the lack of personal contact, and several youth in the study reported that having "someone" to share what was going on in their lives was beneficial.

Developing a Process for Selecting Participants

IRBs are concerned with the fairness of the process by which participants are recruited and selected. Recruitment strategies are expected to be informative and noncoercive. Figure 2.2 summarizes the typical expectations about what will and will not be included in a recruitment strategy. When study participants are known, letters, phone calls, and e-mails of invitation are the typical recruitment strategy. When possible participants are not known, recruitment may be done through agencies, posters, flyers, newspaper ads, television or radio announcements, websites, or Internet ads. Figure 2.3 illustrates what would ordinarily be considered an acceptable poster for recruitment.

Recruitment *should* include:

- Name of investigator
- Identification of research sponsorship (by, e.g., using letterhead)
- Purpose of the research
- How participants will be selected
- Compensation to participants, if any
- Time and other commitments expected
- Contact information for questions or further information

Recruitment *should not* include:

- Suggestive or coercive language (e.g., "earn easy money")
- Misleading information (e.g., "participate in research to cure cancer")

FIGURE 2.2. Requirements for recruitment of study participants.

VOLUNTEERS NEEDED
for a research study

"Understanding the Role of Social Networking Internet Sites in Youth Culture"

The study is open to youth 10 to 18 years of age.

The purpose of the study is to better understand how youth use social networking sites in their interactions with other people.

Participation involves completing a 25-item online survey and a follow-up online interview.

Time commitment: Approximately 1 hour.

The research will be conducted at Big Time University
For additional information, contact Sandra Mathison at: 888-888-8888
or e-mail Sandra at: sm@xxxxxxx

Principal Investigator: Melissa Freeman, PhD
Big Time University, Education Department

FIGURE 2.3. Sample of an acceptable recruitment flyer.

Sometimes the target population is a convenience population and everyone is invited to participate, and so describing how participants will be selected is unnecessary. For example, Blumenreich (2004) was interested in the narratives of children with HIV. At the time of her study, she was director of an advocacy program for children with HIV, and potential participants were children participating in the program.

Sometimes the topic plays a role in who volunteers to participate in a study. In her study of adolescents' attitudes toward the body and menstruation, even though Fingerson (2006) worked with a male partner, approximately two thirds of the teens who chose to participate were female.

Selection of participants is one of the least described processes in descriptions of research methodology. Yet understanding why certain individuals and groups are being chosen and others are not is essential to developing an ethically and methodologically sound research project. IRBs are primarily concerned about the possibility of coercion or breaches of confidentiality in how one identifies and recruits participants for a study, but they are also concerned about how potential participants are informed of their inclusion and exclusion.

For example, we chose fourth- and eighth-grade students for a study on student perceptions of state-mandated testing because, at the time (2003) and in that state (New York), the tests were predominantly given at those grade levels. Had we received more volunteers to participate than we had resources to include, we would have selected individuals to create a diverse group, understanding full well that no one child represents any categorical group, even if he or she shares certain gender or ethnic characteristics. These characteristics do play a role in how individuals are positioned in everyday settings and experience everyday practices so diversity in the population can enable access to diversity of experience. Furthermore, we wanted our student groups to represent as closely as possible the diversity of the schools within which we conducted our study.

However, beyond concerns about confidentiality is the need for researchers to develop an awareness of the social impact of their selection processes. Social constructivist research with children offers an opportunity to hear their views of the kinds of taken-for-granted labels used to classify children. In other words, selecting gifted students for their perceptions of a reading program without also seeking their perspectives on the notion of giftedness and its effects on their daily experiences may serve to reinforce the notion of giftedness as a given, perpetuating its presence in society without consideration for the role it plays in shaping the experiences of those who are included and excluded from its identification. Who is asked to speak shapes our knowledge of a topic in significant ways. For example, in her study of aggression, Simmons (2002) sought ways to talk to a variety of girls between the ages of 10 and 14 whether they had been victims of bullying or victimizers. In this way, she was able to develop a more complex understanding of the relational nature of aggression in the lives of girls rather than single out girls identified as bullies and risk perpetuating a misunderstood stereotype.

Informed Consent from Participants

Are participants able to give informed consent or to read and sign the required document? If not, how will you handle this process? Will parental permission put child participants at more risk than if permission were not sought? If yes, how will you handle this requirement?

Typically, research with youth requires a two-step consent process: obtaining consent from parents or guardians and assent from the youth who will participate in the research. The parental consent is necessary but not sufficient, because the assent by youth themselves allows them to exercise autonomy in choosing whether to participate or not. Although parental consent is considered necessary, there are many circumstances under which children's assent might be waived. For example, if the benefits to children in the study are perceived to be so substantial, the assent requirement might be waived. However, how researchers think about who children are is also an element of assent, and generally a social constructivist researcher would assume that children can and ought to be involved in making a decision about their participation in a research study.

Not only are waivers a possibility, but, depending on the context and circumstances for the research, there is room for multiple interpretations of the kinds of consent and assent that are required. For example, Bogolub and Thomas's (2005) work questions whether the consent of biological parents is always necessary and appropriate. Both conducted research on the experiences of foster children.

Whereas Bogolub, who works in the United States, felt that seeking the written consent of at least one biological parent was essential, Thomas, who works in the United Kingdom, informed the parents of the study but did not seek formal consent. Variations such as these are not uncommon, but they can confuse newcomers to research.

Developing a plan for conducting an ethical and worthwhile project takes time. When we initially planned a study of fourth- and eighth-grade students' perceptions of state-mandated tests in school, our first concern was developing an inviting, clear, and readable set of materials to introduce our study to parents and students. It was when we submitted the material to the university's IRB that inherent contradictions in the IRB guidelines became apparent. Although they understood we were presenting these materials to children and to a diverse group of parents, some of whom did not speak English or read well, and encouraged us to write as clearly and as simply as possible, they returned our forms, requiring us to include information about risk, voluntary status, remuneration for participation, anonymity, selection, storage of information, and confidentiality, including a statement waiving confidentiality if a student shares information that suggests he or she is at risk of being hurt or of hurting others. Finally, we were given approval, but not without a final list of changes we would have to make before proceeding with the study. Figure 2.4 is the message we received from the IRB administrator.

As is clear from this example, the IRB review process is thorough and attempts to identify and prevent every possible misunderstanding or mishap. Simply telling students their parents would not have access to their journals may not have been sufficient had a parent really wanted that access, and it is assumed that putting these statements in writing helps prevent these transgressions from happening. The consequence of these required changes is that our parental permission form took on the appearance of an intimidating legal document with multiple places to check boxes before signing. Because we met with each student to discuss the research process and seek their assent, we were less concerned about the nature of the language on that form than we were about the parental permission form. There is an assumption that, because the form is about their child, parents may look it over more carefully and perhaps see it as an opportunity to expose their child to a new experience. However, a parental sense of protecting their children from strangers, unknown or unclear situations, may also have the opposite effect.

The study is approved pending the following changes:

1. Submit a new permission letter from each school district that documents the participation of the fourth and eighth graders.
2. Resubmit the protocol form cover page in a more readable format.
3. Reduce the compensation to one movie ticket for the fourth graders and one movie ticket plus the bookstore certificate for the eighth graders.
4. Include the child's name on the movie and bookstore vouchers.
5. Revise the collection procedures for the parental consent form and demographic survey to have them mailed to the investigator in a self-addressed envelope. Revise consent form to reflect the change.
6. Revise the letter to the parents to:
   a. Include a statement that the child can withdraw from the study at any time.
   b. Explain the selection criteria, indicating that their child may or may not be selected to participate because of the diverse group that is being sought.
   c. Include information about the demographic survey that parents will be asked to complete.
7. Revise the parental consent to add a statement:
   a. Qualifying confidentiality if information is disclosed that indicates child abuse/neglect or plans to harm oneself or others.
   b. Explaining that the journals of the eighth graders will not be shared with the parents.
   c. Indicating that the child does not have to participate even if the parents give their permission.
   d. Indicating that participants may refuse to answer any question(s) they do not wish to answer (in the "Voluntary Participation" section).
8. Revise the student assent to:
   a. Use more child-friendly language (suggest testing with a fourth grader or a fourth-grade teacher or by using computer software designed to scan for grade-level appropriateness).
   b. Include a statement that the child does not have to participate even if the parent says that she or he can.
   c. Add a statement qualifying confidentiality if information is disclosed that indicates child abuse/neglect or plans to harm oneself or others.

(continued)

FIGURE 2.4. IRB response to consent procedures for a study of children's perceptions of state-mandated testing in school.

---

   d. Add a statement that the journals of the eighth-grade students will not be shared with the parents.

   e. Include a statement indicating that participants may refuse to answer any question(s) they do not wish to answer (in the "Voluntary Participation" section).

9. Include a copy of the "General Directions for Using Your Student Journal" and "Examples of Student Journal Prompts" (Appendix C) with the introductory letter to the parents of the eighth graders.

10. Clarify that the demographic information received from parents whose children are not selected for the study will be destroyed.

11. (...).

12. Revise the procedures for obtaining child assent to have a researcher (not the parents) go over the assent form with each child.

13. Clarify that the master list will be destroyed after data collection is completed.

14. The modification involving students will be considered as a new protocol.

15. (. . .).

16. Clarify that any names or other identifying information that identifies a specific individual in the journals will not be recorded by the researchers.

NOTE: PLEASE REMEMBER THAT BEGINNING THIS RESEARCH PRIOR TO FINAL APPROVAL BY THE INSTITUTIONAL REVIEW BOARD IS A VIOLATION OF UNIVERSITY POLICY AS WELL AS STATE AND FEDERAL REGULATIONS.

FIGURE 2.4. *(continued)*

   The requirement of parental permission is a clear indication of the status and competencies attributed to children. In Western societies especially, parents are understood to be responsible for their children's well-being and that includes deciding what activities are in children's best interests. When parents are asked to give permission for their children to participate in a research project, it is understood that researchers may not decide whether children are capable of making that decision for themselves.

   Research ethics requirements do provide several conditions for waivers of consent or permission, but even with these options decisions about these matters are not straightforward. For example, in their work with children in state custody, Bogolub and Thomas (2005) were informed that seeking the biological parents' permissions was not absolutely necessary. Bogolub ignored this option, however, feeling that bypassing the biological parent would somehow be disrespectful. On the other hand, Thomas, wanting to give the children maximum choice about participating, felt his study would be more ethically and methodologically sound if parental permission was not actively sought. Instead, parents were provided information on the project, which they could then object to, but written consent was not requested. This approach is called "passive consent": Parents are informed about research in which their child is being invited to participate, but a response is required only if the parent objects. This approach is gaining popularity among researchers but is not widely accepted by IRBs (Wagener et al., 2004).

Bogolub and Thomas (2005) concluded that one reason for their differences of practice regarding parental permission is that they are working in very different professional and political contexts. In the United States the attitude toward children is a protectionist one, whereas in the United Kingdom the emphasis is on children's rights, competence, and independence, a movement supported by the 1989 United Nations Convention on the Rights of the Child.

It is important to remember that children occupy a more vulnerable position in society, because adults are still the ones deciding whether permission should be sought. Developing a sound proposal that successfully navigates the regulations for doing social science research is just the first step; it is important to understand that "ethical considerations are ongoing, and that ethical dilemmas may arise at any stage of the research, and not just at the point of contact with research subjects. Further, it is dangerous to assume that because a piece of research has been passed by an ethics committee then it is *ipso facto* an ethical piece of research." (Morrow & Richards, 1996, p. 95)

All research, but perhaps especially research done with children, whether needing IRB approval or not, should consider how the research benefits children, not simply how it furthers adult interests and agendas. Understanding the lived experiences and needs of children is crucial to advocating for their needs at policy and programs level. "Good advocacy depends crucially on a clear and detailed understanding of the situation on the ground" (Roberts, 2000, p. 227). "Since research questions and research agendas are still largely the province of adults, children's narratives tend to be edited, reformulated or truncated to fit our agendas" (Roberts, 2000, p. 229). To keep in mind the obligations to help children through research, researchers should consider the following questions in planning and justifying their research.

1. *What is the purpose of the research?*

   How will research findings benefit children? Who will benefit and how?

2. *What are the potential risks to children?*

   Might there be risks or costs such as time, inconvenience, embarrassment, intrusion of privacy, sense of failure or coercion, or fear of admitting anxiety?

3. *How will anonymity and confidentiality be dealt with?*

   When significant extracts from interviews are quoted in reports, should researchers first check the quotation and commentary with the child (or parent) concerned? How will information about illegal and controversial activities be handled? What safeguards will be in place to avoid false promises of anonymity and confidentiality?

4. *What are the procedures for selection, inclusion, and exclusion?*

   Have some children been excluded because, for instance, they have speech or learning difficulties? Does exclusion deny children a benefit? Can the exclusion be justified?

5. *Are the sources of funding appropriate?*

   Should the research funds be accepted only from agencies that avoid activities that can harm children?

6. *What are the plans for sharing information with children, parents, and other caregivers?*

   Are children and adults given details about the purpose and nature of the research, the methods and timing, and the possible benefits, harms, and outcomes? Is information made available in the native language, in comprehensible ways, in culturally appropriate ways?

7. *How will consent and assent be obtained?*

   Are requests culturally appropriate? Do children know that if they refuse or withdraw from the research, this will not be held against them in any way? How do the researchers help children to know these things?

8. *How will research results be disseminated generally and to study participants?*

Will the children and adults involved be sent reports of the main findings? Are plans for dissemination sensitive to the children's modes of communication?

9. *What impact might the research have on children?*

Besides the effects of the research on the children involved, how might the conclusions affect larger groups of children?

DISCUSSION QUESTIONS

1. Find your organization's human subjects policies, which are usually available on the organization's website. What do they say about working with minors and vulnerable populations? Do they give guidelines about gaining participant assent and parental permission? If so, what are these? What would you add?

2. Develop a parental permission form and a student assent form for a study you are planning. Share it with a classmate. Revise based on feedback.

3. Find an article that is critical of human subjects' procedures, especially as they pertain to working with minors. What aspects of IRB policies and practices is the author most critical of? What are the main arguments? What alternatives are proposed? What is your position on this? Thinking back to Chapter 1, what beliefs about childhood shape your position?

CHAPTER 3

Recruiting Child Participants

> Research is a political activity that involves some form
> of intrusion into people's lives.
> —Barker and Weller (2003, p. 209)

Gaining approval from IRBs is just the beginning of the process of doing research with children. Permission needs to be collected from parents, assent may need to be collected from children, and the actual research design is often negotiated with multiple gatekeepers. In this chapter, we describe the process of seeking parental permission and participant assent and the role these activities can play in the development of rapport between adult researchers and the kids who will eventually participate in a study. Working with gatekeepers to gain access to children is a fundamental part of research with kids and often involves incorporating their views, adapting to institutional schedules and activities, and altering the research design. Within a social constructivist perspective, these processes reveal much about how family members and people in organizations think about children and the way children are situated in our society. We conclude the discussion with an overview of confidentiality issues, a critical aspect of informed consent.

STRATEGIES FOR OBTAINING PARENTAL PERMISSION

Once permission from the IRB and the institutional gatekeepers where the study will be conducted is granted, participants can then be recruited. Unlike adult recruitment, which can be done directly, recruiting child and adolescent participants typically requires parental permission. Unfortunately, as discussed in Chapter 2, the kind of information and the language required by IRBs and the amount of information necessary to include may work against creating an accessible and meaningful message for parents. Working with people who know members of the target community or who can help deliver the information to them is a useful strategy.

When working through an institution, individuals on the inside can often be helpful in the recruitment process. In our study with fourth- and eighth-grade students, we had an established relationship with teachers, administrators, and community workers in the schools where we wished to recruit students. Although we did not use these contacts to connect with parents, we did work with them to begin the research process. This planning process helped in understanding how differences in experience and cultural context might shape the data we eventually collected and influenced the research plan as well. We created packets containing a letter of introduction to parents, a parental permission form, student assent form, and background information form, along with a self-addressed, stamped envelope. We planned to send the packets home with students in their home-school journals. When we contacted the fourth-grade teachers to arrange for the distribution of the packets, the suburban teachers supported our plan, certain we would get a good response. However, the urban teachers expressed skepticism about whether the packets would even make it home. They suggested we talk directly with students and make it clear that only the students who get selected, and therefore had their parents sign and return the forms, would get the compensation of movie tickets we were offering for participating.

As a result of this advice, we opted for the same approach in all four schools. During classroom visits, we explained to the students what our research was about, what the packets contained, what they would need to do to become participants, what they would do as participants, and what they would get in return. We found out that every step of the way gave us information about the context of the study and our potential participants. After visiting the urban fourth-grade classrooms, Freeman wrote in her journal:

> When I mentioned the movie tickets, the students' faces lit up.
> It will be hard to turn down any of these kids if we get too many.
> They had many questions, mainly for me to repeat what I just said.
> But in one classroom an African American boy raised his hand
> and asked, *"Do you think it would be fair if you got the movie tickets and
> then the grown ups took them from you?"* The students turned toward
> me interested in my response. Not sure how to answer, I said, *"No,
> I don't think that would be fair, but do you think that might happen?"*
> Nods of agreement rippled through the students without hesita-
> tion. I realized that if we were to work successfully with such a
> diverse group of students, we would need to adopt a responsive
> and flexible stance toward our research design so as to provide the
> most conducive environment for sharing to occur, but that getting
> the students' feedback on the research process would be equally
> important since it was obvious from this student's statement that
> they had a pretty good understanding of their social situation and
> we had much to learn.

Two weeks later, we received packets from 11 fourth graders in our urban school, 12 in our suburban elementary school, but only four from our suburban and urban middle schools. We included all of the fourth graders and made another recruitment effort with the eighth-grade classrooms. As a result, we recruited six students from the suburban middle school and eight from the urban middle school but lost one of the suburban students during the assent process.

Finding an advocate or confederate within an institution and then making first contact with children within the institutional context is a common practice. Children, like those in our study, demonstrate the ability to ask sensible questions, which can be important data, and this allows them a small amount of privilege in the permissions and assent process. Children are then able to represent to their parents their interest and willingness to participate in a research project as well as answer parent questions.

Another approach is to use the institutional context to make contact with parents. Epstein (1998) describes how she connected with a teacher, Mr. Stuart, who shared her interest in children's gendered cultures. This shared interest encouraged Mr. Stuart to assist with the consent process by writing to parents on the researcher's behalf, explaining who she was and that her research was connected to his curricular focus on "Me, my family and my history."

> Mr. Stuart told the parents that I was researching the ways that boys and girls related to and thought about each other. He also pointed out that the project would include sex education and might give rise to questions about sex and sexuality. Parents were invited to meet with him and me if they had any questions or worries and I promised that I would not record observations of their children if they preferred me not to (no-one took up this offer). (Epstein, 1998, p. 35)

When access to institutions for recruitment purposes is made available, it is important to consider the possible effects the institutional context has on children's ability to make an informed decision about their interest and willingness to participate. For example, in order to recruit elementary and middle-school students to participate in group and individual interviews on parental involvement in education, David, Edwards, and Alldred (2001) distributed flyers and introduced the project to whole classrooms in target schools. Their attempts to present the study directly to children (as opposed to the teachers) did not prevent teachers from giving their opinion about the research study. Several teachers stressed the importance of the research and the value of participating, whereas others suggested who should or should not participate in the research project.

Negotiating access requires the willingness and ability to articulate what your study is about, answer numerous questions from a variety of interested or concerned individuals, and doing so in a way that shows understanding of the nature of the kinds of concerns a teacher, parent, or health clinic staff member might have. During this process, it is important to clarify for gatekeepers how you intend to work with children, what those activities will involve, and who will and who will not have access to the data collected. Negotiating access, however, may also mean convincing your audience of the significance of your study in ways that they can understand. Seeking access to a middle school to recruit African American girls, Evans-Winters (2005), an African American female researcher, found herself facing a white male director of research who first referred to her study as being on student failure even though it was intended to understand their successes and then thought she should study boys instead. By framing the importance of her study in terms of the dropout rates of African American girls, she was given permission. She wrote, "I survived the white man in a suit by using language that most educators and policymakers have become accustomed to hearing, and by embracing patience" (p. 67).

Recruiting youth through institutions is not always successful, however. In their study of children's perceptions of home as a place of risk or safety for children, Hood, Kelley, and Mayall (1996) faced several institutional barriers. First, they tried to gain access to families through a health center, but the health center staff would only agree to distribute a flyer describing the study with a box for potential participants to either check "I agree" or "I don't agree" to be contacted for the study. They received very few responses, so they tried to gain access to parents and children through schools, but the schools would only participate if the study included an educational component that would benefit teachers. From this experience, they concluded that institutional support for research that did not directly contribute to that institutional context was not facilitated by institutional gatekeepers. They also concluded that seeking access to private spaces such as the home was met with resistance: Access into the home was considered intrusive and carried with it an inherent "criticism of the home and its values" (Hood et al., 1996, p. 119).

When researchers find institutions to be restrictive and when the study does not specifically focus on children within a particular institutional context, it may be helpful to use more direct ways to access parents. Recruitment strategies (e.g., posters, e-mail lists, bulletin boards, newspaper ads) described in the previous chapter are appropriate ways to solicit parents' and children's interest in participating in a research project. Parents who respond to such solicitations are already favorably disposed to give their permission for their children's participation in the research study.

If the target research group is known, researchers may use more direct access such as telephone calls or e-mail messages. Barker and Weller (2003) found telephone calls to be straightforward because "parents would either say yes or no so you were negotiating with individuals, not institutions" (p. 212).

These examples of home and school demonstrate the power that gate-keepers wield in terms of affording access to children. In these situations, the researcher often loses autonomy and control of the research. The "politics of access" often requires a lengthy process of negotiation and compromise on the part of the researcher, as they liaise through entire complex networks of gatekeepers before asking a child whether he or she would like to participate. (Barker & Weller, 2003, p. 213)

When the focus of a research study may predispose parents and guardians to deny permission to access children as research participants, extraordinary strategies may be needed. For example, child participation in studies of violence against and abuse of children may not be permitted, especially if the perpetrators of violence and abuse are the parents or guardians. In such cases, the value of the research to generate insights and solutions that will improve the quality of life for the specific children or all children may justify an access strategy that circumvents parents and guardians as the typical first step of obtaining permission.

GETTING KIDS TO PARTICIPATE AFTER YOU ARE "IN"

The view that childhood is a social construction alters our understanding (and reveals our lack of understanding) of children, their capabilities, and linguistic competencies. In Chapter 1, we discussed how conceptions of children made it more likely that they would be seen as the object of research, perhaps having children completing objective tasks or tests; interviewing parents, teachers, and other adult observers of children; or conducting observations of specific behaviors rather than seeing children as legitimate interpreters of their own lives. Adopting a social constructivist view, however, does not prevent prevalent social views from having an effect on our perceptions. Child participants in research are conceptualized in a number of ways:

- The *innocent child* needing protection;
- The *deprived disadvantaged child* needing resources and services;
- The *criminal child* requiring control;
- The *ignorant child* needing education;
- The *excluded child* who may need special shelter or opportunities;

- The *disabled child* who is the victim of personal tragedy or of a rejecting society; and

- The *strong resourceful child* who can work with adults towards solving problems and creating new opportunities. (Alderson, 2005, p. 30)

In the age of children as passive receptors of an adult society, assent was not required, but a social constructivist view acknowledges children's rights and the legitimacy of their own accounts. It also advocates vigilance in attending to the way one or more of the prior conceptions of children may affect a researcher's relationship to children in the course of the research study. Each of these conceptions implies a certain relationship between researcher and child and influences how the researcher values and integrates his or her perspective into the data analysis and interpretation. Keeping a researcher journal of impressions, thoughts, and interpretations is a good way to document research activities and decisions as well as reflect on preconceived notions about the research topic and participants and the ways in which research participants contribute to or alter those perceptions.

Parental permission gives the researcher the go-ahead to ask kids if they wish to participate in a study. Although children's assent is not always necessary, it is increasingly the norm and indeed quite consistent with a social constructivist or a strong resourceful child perspective that children be permitted to exercise control in deciding whether they wish to participate in a research study. In general, researchers should create the conditions for a child to give permission that promote meaningful and informed participation, including

- Clear explication of what the purpose of the research is and a genuine commitment to listen to and take children seriously.

- Assurances that children's participation is voluntary and relevant to them.

- Child-centered ways of working together that affirm and maintain positive self-esteem and confidence, including child-friendly spaces and language.

- Statements that ensure the safety of children, including issues of confidentiality and anonymity, respect for personal boundaries, and not putting children at risk of physical or psychological harm.

■ Efforts to appropriately involve children in decision making about the research process, including criteria about who will participate and what forms of data collection and reporting make the most sense.

Age has often been viewed as a determining factor in seeking assent from children. In the last decade, however, different interpretations of what can be understood as children's competence have arisen, especially in medicine regarding a young person's right to consult privately with a doctor independent of parental consent (Morrow & Richards, 1996). It is now more likely that multiple factors are taken into account when determining a child's capacity for consent. For example, "age, general cognitive ability, emotional status and knowledge" are important factors (Lindsay, 2000, p. 12). Others take a more interactive and contextual approach.

> Perhaps searching for a minimum threshold age for children's consent is asking the wrong question. Depending on the context and the complexity of the judgment, children at most ages are capable of making decisions concerning what they want to do, so perhaps the child's competency to consent to research participation should not be regarded as an inflexible limitation deriving from the child's age, but rather as an interaction of the child, the context, and the nature of the (decision-making) task. Children from a surprisingly early age can understand basic elements of the research process and their role within if this information is presented in an age-appropriate manner. (Thompson, 1992, p. 60)

From this perspective, giving assent or consent is not just a matter of children's capacity to understand, but of the researcher's talent in conveying a clear and detailed account of what participating in the study entails. It is equally important to convey the message to children that participating is their choice and they can say no. Studies of children's talk reveal that children younger than 6 years can formulate hypothetical "What if" statements; children as young as 3 will ask for more information if they are unclear of something, and 4-year-olds will offer alternative suggestions if they disagree with peers. Children are less likely to do these things with adults, however, because they are taught that they should defer to adult knowledge or that they should not argue, disagree, or negotiate meanings with

adults (Coles, 1996). Children may interpret the request to participate from many different angles, including a position of feeling powerless to say no to one of feeling empowered by the request for their
participation.

Therefore, part of the process of seeking assent for a study should
involve modeling the child's right to ask clarifying questions or to say
no. For example, although Holmes (1998) did not seek assent from
the children in her study, she did feel that it was important to make
clear their rights as participants:

> I have always supplied the children with an explanation about my proj-
> ects that is developmentally appropriate. On the first day of class, I
> invite the children to sit on the floor with me in a circle. At this time,
> I explain the project to them. I answer any questions they may have
> about the project or my presence in their class. I tell them that there
> are no right or wrong answers to any of the questions I may ask them,
> and that they do not have to participate in activities if they do not wish
> to. (p. 16)

Seeking assent is likely the first personal contact with child or
adolescent participants. Rather than view this process simply as an
ethical obligation, it is also an important first meeting with research
participants (maybe your only one-on-one meeting depending on
the data-collection strategies). Therefore, researcher demeanor, the
questions the researcher asks, and the way the researcher comports
herself all play a role in establishing rapport and building trust. It
can also affect the research practice, as we have found in our own
research.

In our testing study, we decided our explanation of the research
project should describe what we planned to do in our focus groups,
describe why we were interested in young people's perspectives,
and share a little about ourselves as researchers and what it means
to be a researcher. We also planned to ask the students questions
about themselves, their families, their contact information, and how
they got back and forth from school. This excerpt from Freeman's
research journal discusses this process:

> We met with the suburban fourth graders. One by one we fetched
> a student out of his or her classroom, walked over to a private
> cubby in the library to go over the project and assent form. This

group of students ranged from shy to talkative but they knew their phone numbers and addresses, live at home with two parents, go regularly to the movies, and clearly knew their after-school schedules. For the most part, they felt that meeting after school would work best except we would have to schedule our days so that they didn't interfere with other extracurricular events. The principal agreed that meeting after school would be the best plan.

What a contrast meeting the urban students. Again, their demeanor ranged from shy to talkative, but, unlike the suburban students, many of these students live with one parent or live between two homes like an aunt and parent or a grandmother and parent. Most walk home with friends or family. Many were unsure of their address, several did not have phones, most did not attend any after-school programs, few had ever gone to the movies, and those who did reported needing to take the bus. Furthermore, several of the students do not speak English as their first language.

Because of this, we became very concerned with our plan to meet the students after school. Not only were we concerned that getting parents to sign an extra permission slip might cause us to lose some participants, but we were mostly concerned that students might need to walk home in the dark after our meetings. When we shared our concerns with a teacher, he suggested that we meet during school hours. We decided that that was a good idea.

Assent provides an opportunity to discuss a research project with participants, allowing them to make a more informed decision about participation. We repeated the process with our eighth-grade students. This was a simple process of going to the classroom where students were located and inviting them to come out and talk with us one by one or in small groups. When one of the urban eighth-grade boys was invited to talk with us, he was taken aback and was even more surprised when he found out that his mother had signed and returned the forms. He was assured that he did not have to sign up but we reminded him what we were asking the students to do, that he could give it a try, and if he was uncomfortable or uninterested he could drop out at any time. He asked how many students had signed up. We told him seven, and he said he would try it. A similar conversation happened with a boy recruited in the suburban middle school, but in this case he explained that he was not at all interested in participating and withdrew from the study.

Even with the best of intentions, however, explaining the scope and purpose of a study to young people may not meet the degree of information that would be considered "informed." Epstein (1998) showed children her researcher tools, such as her notebook, and allowed them to choose their own pseudonyms. Reflecting on this process, she concluded the children did not understand the consequences that may arise from being a participant in a study. For example, allowing the children to pick their own pseudonym created breaches of confidentiality because they often picked the name of their best friend or were heard telling their teacher what pseudonym they had chosen for themselves. Epstein agreed she would show the school principal what she had written before publication, but she became concerned that some of the children were easily identifiable through their activities and descriptions. She determined the children in her study could not have given their consent from an informed position because they did not understand the kinds of consequences that could arise from being identified in a research report. Epstein's experience suggests researchers consider two questions:

1. Is the research important enough to justify when children's capacity for informed consent may be limited in any way?
2. Has every effort to explain the research to the children been made so that their consent will be as informed as possible?

Children need to be informed of their rights as participants in concrete, action-centered ways. Figure 3.1 is one example of a list of rights that could be shared with children to clarify their role.

When seeking assent in person is not possible, it becomes even more important to convey the scope and purpose of the study and why the perceptions of children matter. In their study of children's perceptions of the home as a place of risk or safety, Hood et al. (1996) asked parents to discuss the research with their child and seek his or her agreement to participate.

> This sometimes resulted in parents reporting their child's refusal. However, we did not and we could not directly approach children to seek their consent until our visit to the family home. It remains an uncom-

It is for you to decide if you want to participate.

Before you decide whether to help me, you might like to talk about this project with your parents or a friend.

You can take time to decide if you want to participate; don't rush to make a decision.

You do not have to say yes.

If you do say yes, you can change your mind at any time.

If you say no, you do not need to give a reason.

If you say no, you will not be punished in any way.

We can stop, or take a break, when you want to.

If you do not want to answer questions or participate in activities, you can just say pass.

I keep tapes and notes of the interviews in a safe place.

When I talk about my research and write reports, I change people's names to keep their views anonymous.

I would not talk to anyone you know about what you have said, unless you talk about the risk of someone being harmed. If so, I would talk with you first about what could be done to help.

FIGURE 3.1. Research participants' *Bill of Rights.* Based on Alderson (2004).

fortable irony that in this research *with* children, we could successfully access them only by negotiating within the accepted framework of the "hierarchy of gate keeping." Conversely, children's ability to refuse to participate took place within their social positioning as inferiors not only to their parents but to us, the researchers. (p. 121)

Examples such as these are reminders that research is a social activity that is embedded in larger social and cultural traditions and relationships, and we discuss this relational aspect of research further in Chapter 4.

CONFIDENTIALITY

The complex issue of confidentiality is made more complex when participants are children and adolescents and made even more so in particular institutional contexts such as prisons, hospitals, and even schools. Although the offer of anonymity and confidentiality is taken for granted in the research process, it is not straightforward and promises of confidentiality necessarily have a limited reach, about which researchers must be frank. The key is to realistically outline the particular conditional nature of confidentiality for a given research study. Generally, however, protection of life and safety will at some point override the commitment to confidentiality, although disclosure must be governed by a continued commitment to safeguard the rights and interests of research participants.

Parents and other gatekeepers view children's worlds as their business. This belief can range from helpful interventions to ones that seek to monitor, and even control, children's activities. For example, we limited the use of a take-home journal for students to record their impressions of state testing to eighth-grade study participants. We did not perceive fourth-grade participants as less capable of keeping a journal; rather, it was because of our understanding of parents' perceptions of their role in relation to children's "school" activities. We felt there was a significant chance the journal would be perceived as homework and parents might assume they should monitor whether their child was accomplishing that task. Barker and Weller (2003) asked children to take photographs of specific spaces in their communities and found some parents had taken the pictures for their 4- to 11-year-old children. With older children, 13 to 16 years of age, this did not happen. In these cases, ensuring confidentiality is difficult because the research activities encroach on the activities of other spaces such as the home. As we discuss in Chapter 6, conducting interviews in the home presents its own set of issues; for example, interviews in the home are often conducted in the presence of a parent, which necessarily affects the researcher–participant relation and the data generated (Barker & Weller, 2003). In fact, seeking to meet with children individually can be threatening to parents because it can be perceived as altering the parent–child hierarchy and using children as informants against parents (Hood et al., 1996).

The expectation that others may want access to data arises in most institutional settings and so must be viewed in light of issues of confidentiality. This interest may be made explicit during negotiations for access to children in institutional contexts, such as a principal wanting access to data out of concern for how the school may be portrayed, or it may arise as a result of data-collection procedures. First, clarity of the research purpose and scope is essential to communicate to gatekeepers, as is the necessity of negotiating up-front who will have access to what data, in what form, and under what circumstances. It is common practice, for example, to disclose information shared by young people if that information leads the researcher to worry about the safety of particular people. In these cases, researchers disagree about the correct course of action, some preferring to discuss the issue directly with the participant and disclosing such information with others only if the child agrees (Alderson, 1995), and others preferring to discuss the issue with an adult such as a counselor who is perceived as having the expertise in such matters. Regardless, young persons need to be made aware during the assent process that this kind of information may not be kept confidential if they were to share it.

Second, the researcher should pay attention to the ways in which methods put confidentiality at risk. Large-scale studies often involve many people in the research process, especially during data collection. Increased numbers of people with access to data simply means more chances that confidentiality may be breached. When the go-between for data collection is someone with a prescribed role in relation to children, such as a teacher or nurse or social worker, that role may void promises of confidentiality. For example, Wheelock, Babell, and Haney (2000) had teachers collect drawings from students, which were then sent to the researchers. The images drawn by the children were not anonymous, and many points of potential breach of confidentiality are created when gatekeepers are also data collectors. Barker and Weller (2003) had students complete questionnaires about their use of off-limit spaces. Many of the responses were scribbled over, leading the researchers to wonder whether this was related to the teacher's role in data collection. A teacher commented he had looked through the questionnaires to see whether the students were answering it properly, leading the researchers to rethink this approach. Rather than eliminate the questionnaire, children were provided a sticky label with which to seal their survey form when completed.

Research that involves visual methods, particularly videography and photography, require special consideration regarding anonymity and confidentiality. When the visual images become part of reporting the results of a study, and indeed the visual images may be necessary to communicate children's meaning and experience, either honest admission that confidentiality cannot be ensured or ways to ensure confidentiality must be built in from the beginning of the study. Photographs, for example, can be "redrawn" as line figures, altered to make faces fuzzy, or presented with low pixel counts as a way to use visual images but maintain children's anonymity.

Discussion of access and consent processes set the stage for critical questions about the stances that researchers working with children take, such as adopting "least-adult" (Mandell, 1991a) roles or viewing children as the same as adults. We address these issues in Chapter 4.

DISCUSSION QUESTIONS

1. Look at the list of conceptualizations of children on pages 42–43. Which ones are most likely to come to mind when you think of young children? What about adolescents? Reflect on where these images come from and which ones would be most difficult for you to change. Share your reflection with a classmate. How different are your assumptions? Discuss reasons for these differences.

2. Develop a short introductory narrative for gatekeepers, explaining the nature and purpose of your study. Include the nature and expectations of your relationship with gatekeepers, how you will contact potential participants, how you will seek out their assent and their parents' permissions, what kind of data you hope to generate, and the kind of reporting you plan to do.

3. Write an access memo of your experiences gaining access to child participants. Consider writing the memo in the genre of a travel log as though describing the places and people you met along the way to someone foreign to the context where you are conducting your study. What kind of assumptions did you take for granted in the process? What new awareness was gained?

CHAPTER 4

Defining Researcher Roles in Research with Children

> Because interpretive research comes out of interactions among
> people, role construction is an ongoing process. Needs of
> participants shift over time as conditions change, physical
> demands shift, and relationships build, rupture, and are repaired.
> Role negotiation occurs repeatedly over the course of a study.
> —GRAUE AND WALSH (1998, p. 76)

Co-constructing meaning with children and adolescents begins
during the initial recruitment effort, as described in Chapter 3,
and continues throughout the duration of the research and even
beyond as researchers continue to engage with the words, images,
and impressions—the data—left behind by children. Researching
children's experience usually involves negotiating the nature of the
child–researcher contact both with children and the adults responsible for them. Negotiations with adults may revolve around the need
for space and time with participants, and these needs (such as for
privacy and confidentiality) are not always clear to adult gatekeepers. Central to the process of co-constructing meaning with child
participants is developing a social relationship between a researcher
and participants within a social context.

We discuss here the importance of relationships, whether they develop over time as researchers spend considerable time with children as participant observers or need to be quickly established when researchers and children first get together for interviews, focus groups, or other formal data-collection activities. Context, beliefs about children, and their beliefs about adults shape expected adult–children relationships, and these in turn affect the researcher–participant interaction. This discussion concludes with an overview of different methodologies and their advantages and disadvantages when working with children and adolescents.

THE EFFECT OF INSTITUTIONS ON RESEARCHER ROLES

Although much research is conducted by teachers in their own classrooms or psychologists on their own practices, the focus here is on research conducted with children unknown to the researcher before the study and in settings where permission is needed for access. We focus here on the challenges of building rapport with children in settings such as homes and schools where adults are perceived to act in specific ways, ways that may not be conducive to eliciting rich information from children.

One condition of working with children is that researchers generally have little control over the settings in which contact with children will occur. Sometimes these spaces are conducive to individual or group-based activities because they offer privacy and adequate space, tables for drawing, or rugs or couches for gathering. Other times the space is small and uninviting or loud and lacking privacy. Some researchers seek to meet children in their own homes, where the presence of adults or other children can become a distraction and interfere with some kinds of data collection. Negotiating space within these settings becomes an important consideration. This often means reminding others of the nature of the study and the need for privacy. Finding private spaces in view of others is often possible in the back of rooms, out in the garden, or by leaving doors open and letting people know they can drop in anytime (Morrow & Richards, 1996).

Furthermore, the settings themselves, and how they are used, carry with them particular rules and norms of behavior, action, and interaction. For example, we conducted focus groups with urban fourth graders in the family resource room during school hours, whereas we met with the suburban fourth graders after school hours in a classroom. The relaxed, playroom nature of the family room was conducive to multiple activities such as drawing and small-group work, but meeting during school hours may have encouraged children to view our activities as school related rather than research related. In contrast, meeting after school fostered a positive club-like atmosphere, but it also meant that our group was competing with other possible desirable activities, such as hanging out with friends.

Institutionalized spaces, which are designed and monitored by adults, not only embody certain cultural and social norms over others, but they also reinforce certain modes of relating at the exclusion of others (Barker & Weller, 2003; James et al., 1998). For example, running around and climbing the jungle gym with 2- to 4-year-olds helped Mandell (1991a) build a researcher–participant relationship she felt was nonthreatening and gave her entry into the children's culture. Participant observation studies have the advantage of working within children's everyday spaces. They have the disadvantage of being imbued with their own notions of power and authority, inclusion and exclusion, and child and adult roles and responsibilities. Prioritizing contact with children, therefore, often occurs at the expense of other relationships and within contexts and cultures that hold certain expectations for adult and child behaviors. Mandell (1991a), Corsaro (1981), Epstein (1998), and Thorne (1993), although not necessarily agreeing on the roles one should take in relation to children, describe challenges of negotiating access to children's worlds as participant-observer adults. Researchers may feel a discomfort with being perceived as odd by both adults and children and the tension of maintaining a primary position in the children's world when adults in the situation could clearly use some "adult" help. Wanting to understand and emphasize how children negotiate and interpret experience requires an approach that assumes the researcher's ability to experience those cultural interactions as a child would; adult perspectives are suspended in an effort to experience the child's world as a child.

Children do not passively reproduce social structures and processes, but their behaviors toward and expectations of others such as adult researchers or other child participants reflect, in part, their positions within those institutions. For example, children are generally taught early on to take directions from adults, to see adults as figures of authority and knowledge and not, for example, as playmates or equals.

Institutions tend to promote specific conceptions of children. For example, the practice of grouping children by age in schools embodies the notion of the socially developing child described in Chapter 1. These structures, in turn, influence the design of research studies.

> To what extent, for example, are we led to design our research with the age stratification of the school in mind and what implications might this have for our research? Would findings about sexuality, gender, ethnicity, friendship, bullying, play and work, for example, look different if they had been gathered outside the context of the school or other child-specific, age-based institutions such as youth-clubs or day-care centres? (James et al., 1998, p. 176)

The context influences how children behave, and it also influences how researchers negotiate their role in these contexts. Researchers bring their own biography to a study, and that biography is important in managing who they will be in the research context. For example, many researchers are parents or former teachers or nurses, and so there is a natural pull to fall into those adult roles. Children understand adults in those roles better than an adult-as-researcher role and so implicitly encourage those roles in the developing relationships. Additionally, the structure of the research context has prescribed roles for adults. In schools, for example, adults are there to instruct, care for, comfort, and control children. The researcher may well find her- or himself working against the familiar in order to get at children's meanings and experiences. "As a researcher one can resist these discourses but it is impossible to refuse them completely or to step right outside of them, partly because the expectations of both children and other adults are so strongly organized through the discourses of adult-as-teacher" (Epstein, 1998, p. 30).

Understanding the institutional role assigned to adults within the research context is critical to planning the role of adult as researcher working with children. In schools, for example, there are places that children are not permitted to go, like the teachers' lounge, that signal to children that adults are allowed private space away from children, but that children are not given any private spaces away from adults. If a researcher occupies that adult-only space, children will see the researcher as an adult and possibly less connected to them as children. Sensitivity to the cultural norms of the context is also important: Doing research in aboriginal communities, for example, will require acknowledging and working with the conception of adults as respected elders, deserving of deference and respect. Depending on the specific research context, these typical adult roles may be quite obvious, whereas in others it may be helpful to engage in some unstructured, nonparticipant observation before beginning to do research with children.

However, an intention to do research with children and to do so within institutional structures ultimately requires the researcher to "take sides" (Becker, 1967), not in the sense of advocacy or sentimentality but in the sense of building trust with both children and adults in the context in order to maximize access to the lived experiences of children. Just as researchers make claims about the generalizability of their work, so should we be clear that social constructivist research with children is research through the eyes of children rather than, for example, through the eyes of parents, teachers, or medical staff. The weight one gives to the children's own interpretation of these voices in the final analysis depends on the role a researcher gives to theory, but the building blocks for a critical or feminist perspective lie in the accounts of the children, and so it is these accounts that take precedence.

Simultaneously, researchers should explore their own biography regarding the roles of adults and children within the particular research context, an especially important task when the context is one the researcher has lived through. Schools are the most common place to find children and even if the research is not related to schooling or education, schools are frequently the site for recruitment and data collection. Although adult researchers may believe their experiences in schools are in the past and not relevant to the research moment, their own experiences of schooling will well up within that context. Was the researcher a good student perceived positively by teachers or a troublesome student frequently in the principal's office? Was the researcher a participator or leader or a follower or alienated? There are, of course, other aspects of biography that matter in developing a researcher role with children: Traits such as age, size, ethnicity, gender, and disposition are also considerations. When Evans-Winters (2005) sought permission to recruit African American girls in an urban middle school for her study on resiliency, she was surprised with how nervous the principal's office made her feel in contrast to her general confidence meeting the director of research:

> In junior high school (now referred to as middle school), I spent as much time in the principal's office getting reprimanded or suspended as I did picking up an honor roll certificate or running errands for a teacher. Therefore, I was more nervous about approaching the schools' principal than I had been about confronting a white man in a suit. (p. 67)

PRESENTATION OF SELF AS RESEARCHER

How researchers present themselves to participants, the beliefs researchers have about children (who embody diversity because of, e.g., age, ethnicity, language, culture, interests, personality), and how researchers (who also embody multiple demographic and personality traits) are perceived by children play a role in fostering or hampering the researcher–participant relationship. Self-reflexivity is important to explore one's assumptions about children because decisions about how to seek access and relate within the research context are influenced by what we expect of children. The role we assume in our relationship with children is shaped by these beliefs and by what we hope to achieve (i.e., be seen as genuinely trustworthy, caring, and interested). It is also shaped by children's other experiences with adults, their class, gender, ethnicity, and age.

For example, whereas we felt confident that eighth graders understood that adults held different role identities and that in our relationship with them we were researchers, even if we might be parents or teachers in our relationship with others, we were less certain of how well the fourth graders understood this. Their age and more limited experience with a variety of adults and the fact that we met with them at their school and asked them to engage in a variety of tasks meant that it was more likely they assessed their relationship with us as more similar than different to that of a teacher, which may have affected how they understood their rights as participants. At 9 years of age, they probably felt more compelled to do what we asked because they believed that we might punish or scold them, like other adults they encounter daily, if they did not. Although we did not, and would not have, punished the children for misbehaving or refusing to participate, we did encounter situations that required some sort of corrective action on our part in order to keep the group process working. These situations, in turn, contribute to maintaining adult–child power differences, a topic we address in Chapter 5.

As we describe in Chapter 1, adults hold a variety of beliefs about children. We take a social constructivist perspective because we believe that meaning and understanding about self and others are constructed in the interactions we have with our participants. Furthermore, these interactions are shaped by the social contexts children and researchers inhabit, their prior experiences, and the way they understand the expectations of the research relationship. Meaning is necessarily seen as being a construction because children, as interpretive agents, are responding and participating in the tasks, questions, and activities put forth by researchers and others. Believing this, we, for example, structured group interviews using multiple methods, integrating spoken, written, and artistic responses, a topic we return to later in this chapter. Providing multiple approaches gave the students numerous opportunities to express their thoughts and share their experiences in ways that built on individual differences and styles of interaction.

Beliefs about children shape the way researchers design their studies and the kinds of methods they use. Researchers who believe that children inhabit a distinct culture separate from adults or who want to emphasize the effect a social or institutional context has on the lived experiences of young people (the tribal or social structural child), for example, tend to emphasize participant observation as a primary data-collection method (James et al., 1998). The assumption is that children inhabit a separate world or, if not an entirely separate one, that the world children perceive is inaccessible to adults, at least within adult structures. To gain access necessitates close observation and participation over time. The primary focus is on how children, through their verbal and physical interactions, games, songs, conversations, behaviors, routines, and so on, construct a cultural space and how in turn that space shapes the way they interact and behave. The advantage of participant observation is that it allows the researcher to observe the actions and interactions of children as they occur. "By carefully entering the worlds of children and youth and charting the historicity of significant aspects and phases of their lives, ethnographers can document crucial changes and transitions that are essential for understanding socialization as a process of production and reproduction" (Eder & Corsaro, 1999, p. 522).

Even within this conception of children, there are a number of roles an adult may assume: adult as friend, adult as peripheral participant, adult as child. Although there are disagreements about what adult roles are possible and genuine, in general, the goal is to take a least-adult role (Mandell, 1991a), that is, a role that aligns the researcher more (in language and behavior) with children than with adults. Although adult researchers cannot be children, adopting a role should suspend as much as possible the adult role, in much the same way as other partisan roles are suspended in the research process (Fine & Sandstrom, 1988; Waksler, 1991). The researcher role may then be manifest as a peripheral participant (Corsaro, 1996) or an adult friend. These roles require the researcher to differentiate themselves from typical adult roles so as to gain access to the peer relations and child interactions. These least-adult roles are best described by Mandell:

> Following the children's ways, by doing what they did, and by becoming involved with them on a daily basis, I was able to gain an understanding of their thoughts and actions. Specifically I focused on small (two to three) groups of children and literally followed them around their play space. If they sat in the sandbox making cakes, so did I. If they scrambled up the climbers, crawled under the porch or chased each other around the yard as "Superman," I followed. While I did not "become a child," I nonetheless became as "minimally adult" as possible. This required that I neither judge nor evaluate their actions, nor act as a nurturing nor authoritative teacher. While the children initially attempted to engage me in a teacher's role, with consistent refusal their demands subsided. They taught me their openers, rules for entry, procedure and exit from interaction and I, in turn, demonstrated who I was to be to them. Naturally the latter involved considerable testing of my neutrality, confidentiality and physical dexterity. However in time they either forgot I was there or engaged me fully in their activities. (1991b, p. 165)

This nonauthoritative, child-like role seeks to actively see what the world looks like from a child's perspective by acting out that perspective. Perhaps the most difficult balance in establishing a researcher role is to be genuine. Clearly, pretending to be a child when you are not is misleading; however, informing children that you want to know what it is like to be a child so when you are with them you are going to pretend to be a child is not. Children are capable interpreters of their world and will probably take pride in showing a researcher "the way" when the relationship is negotiated openly with children. The challenge for researchers who adopt a tribal view "is to find some way of tapping into the private and autonomous social world of childhood in order to come to grips with the forms and practices of this world" (Ball, 1985, p. 48).

Researchers who adopt the least-adult role understand, however, that adopting any role before their contact with children as an attempt to alter children's perceptions of them is an imposition rather than a negotiation (Epstein, 1998). Adults who take on least-adult roles make a commitment not to interfere in the research setting, which raises ethical issues if researchers observe interactions among children that have the potential or likelihood of leaving someone harmed. It is inevitable that researchers will experience interactions, behavior, and discourse that may appear or be unacceptable in an adult world. Anticipating such disconnections is helpful in creating and sustaining a least-adult role. For example, in her study of middle-school youth, Eder witnessed children abusing others. Sometimes she diverted attention away from the abusing situation but questioned whether she should have intervened more actively, suggesting that nonintervention may actually decrease "young people's perceptions of adults as responsible advocates on their behalf" (Eder & Corsaro, 1999, p. 527).

The stance one takes cannot be easily predetermined, will affect the researcher's relationships with participants, and needs to be taken into account in the analysis. For example, Morris-Roberts (2001) describes how her study of 14- and 15-year-old teenage girls' friendship groups led her to align herself with one group at the exclusion of other girls. She found herself caught between wanting to put into practice a feminist stance that aimed at providing voices for marginalized experiences and intervening when exclusionary practices occurred and finding herself complicit of these exclusionary practices when she found herself admitted into one friendship group, which necessarily involved excluding others.

Acting ethically is not simply a role-based or age-determined characteristic but a way of presenting one's self in a social context. Not intervening in situations in which a child is getting hurt may threaten children's overall perception of the researcher as an individual and reduce their trust in his or her judgment and interest in them or, as Morris-Roberts' example shows, result in deepening one's access to some participants often at the expense of others. On the other hand, reprimanding children for swearing or being silly or inattentive may serve to reproduce their conception of the researcher as an adult rather than a friend with whom they can share their experience. Nonintervention can also reflect the researcher's belief in the capabilities of children and young people to work things out for themselves and be based on faith in their abilities rather than assuming that adults have the know-how to intervene. Finally, nonintervention can send young participants the message that you are interested and willing to follow them wherever they take you, regardless of how much you agree or disagree with the world they show you. Simmons (2002) feels that the success of her study on the culture of aggression in girls was her ability to listen nonjudgmentally and to go wherever the girls wanted to take her.

Not all researchers who approach the study of children through participant observation take on a tribal view of the child. Adults who assume a social or socially constructed view of the child view children as competent participants in an adult-developed world. The focus is not on the world children construct but on the way children participate in, make sense of, and, through their actions and interactions, alter the world they share with adults. "Children do not merely internalize individually the external adult culture. Rather, they become part of adult culture—that is, contribute to cultural reproduction and change—through their negotiations with each other and their production of a series of peer cultures with other children" (Eder & Corsaro, 1999, p. 520). Unlike, taking on an "adult child" perspective, in which children are viewed as having the same competencies as adults, the social and socially constructed conceptions suggest that children are competent social actors with different competencies, perspectives, and experiences.

Regardless of which conception of children is adopted, they are not equals in society. Children are positioned in society such that adult researchers will be perceived as having greater power in relation to children. One of the first steps in establishing a collaborative relationship or one that works to minimize power differences is the informed consent process. Understanding that they can choose not to participate or that they can withdraw at any time is an essential part of the process for children or adolescents who do not always have an opportunity to make choices about participating. Although children are often perceived as lacking maturity, cognitive development, or essential abilities, it is important not to construct deficiencies that are not there. Children come to the research situation with predetermined skills and abilities, and the researcher should investigate what those skills and abilities in the particular research context are and meet children where they are cognitively and linguistically. Doing so should not undermine children's abilities to interpret and alter their language in new situations. Children will, like all social beings, alter their style to match the situation. Children will also test new situations, for example, by cursing or refusing to do a task, to see what the researcher will do; in this way, children test what we want from them while also checking out who we are as individuals.

Similarly, who we are as researchers will enable or constrain the kinds of relationships we are able to have with our participants. Carter (2005), an African American female researcher exploring the beliefs and aspirations of African American and Latino teenagers, although feeling that she had built good rapport through participant observation, hired a male researcher to conduct the focus groups with male participants. She explained that there was good reason to believe the male teenagers would not act authentically with a female moderator in the presence of their peers. In contrast, Davidson (1996), a European American female researcher investigating the ethnic identity formation of African American, European American, Latino, and Vietnamese high school sophomores, was often questioned as to her ability to understand these students' lives. She admits that being a female restricted her ability to follow the boys as many places as the girls and that not being able to speak the many languages her participants spoke restricted her access in different ways, but she feels the 3 years she spent with them in their school greatly compensated for these gaps.

Children are social because they live social lives. The child is seen as a competent respondent of his or her experience in this shared world, shared because they are always in contact with adults but different because their perspective of this contact is necessarily shaped by their position within it. These beliefs about children lead to the use of multiple methods, often combining traditional methods such as participant observation and interviewing with more innovative methods such as incorporating activities, drawing, or photography into the interviews or the overall methodological design. A move away from the traditional question-and-answer format not only helps to lessen the power imbalances found between adults and children (Punch, 2002b), but it fosters and supports multiple forms of expression, an approach that may be valuable with adult participants as well.

Multiple methods also support the communicative styles that children who inhabit different race, gender, and class positions may have while also altering preconceived perceptions children may have of researchers, who may also come with different gender, class, and race characteristics. Relationships are developed through activities, through acting together in ways that foster communication and trust; therefore, researchers, especially if they do not look like adults with whom children have daily contact, need to pay attention to how they are presenting themselves to child participants and, in turn, how the children seem to be responding to them.

Researching children's experiences requires us to educate children about research and what it means to participate in a research project as participants or, as we discuss in Chapter 10, as coresearchers. Failures of understanding should not automatically be considered evidence that children lack social or communicative skills. Children may be less responsive than adult participants, but this may be for a variety of reasons (e.g., researcher's inability to clearly describe the purpose and focus of the research interaction, or a study topic that is not interesting to children).

The issue of negotiating what it means to participate in research is rarely addressed beyond the consent and assent process in the literature. Research is an adult practice, and researchers rarely address how children's understanding of the research process affects their style of interaction and participation. "Kids' understandings of the research process itself have . . . been almost completely ignored. Indeed, the assumption seems to be that researchers get better data if those understandings are kept intentionally incomplete: Researchers are encouraged to be marginal, least adults who specify only vague goals" (Nespor, 1998, p. 373).

Using different methods should enrich the study by generating multiple entry points for answering the research question. This includes considering what traditional methods such as participant observation and interviewing can offer as well as more innovative approaches such as photoelicitation interviewing or alternative forms of writing. Methods should always generate useful and relevant data and not merely be fun or gimmicky (Punch, 2002b, p. 330). Interviewing, for example, can assist in understanding how children make sense of events and experiences, whereas participant observation may be useful in understanding how events take shape and how they affect different actors, in ways these actors may not even be aware of. Spending time observing children can enhance an interview study by provoking questions that adult researchers may not automatically have about children's experiences and can help researchers put into context the experiences children share during interviews. Group and individual interviews, in turn, can assist participant observers by helping them attend to events of significance to the children. In our work, we found it very helpful to have spent time in each setting observing daily events and different interpersonal interactions before conducting focus groups with fourth- and eighth-grade children. The rapport that is built during interviews, by showing interest in their thoughts and experiences or during participant observation through one's presence and attention, can create researcher–participant relationships that engage child participants and give them the means to express themselves in multiple ways.

Research with children can, of course, use any extant social science research methods; however, a social constructivist approach will favor data-collection methods that allow children to co-construct meaning with the researcher. Methods that adopt an a priori framework, such as survey techniques, standardized interviews, checklists, and tests of psychological traits, are not typical within this research perspective. Instead, methods that give children shared control of the language and concepts are favored. Figure 4.1 gives an overview of data-collection methods used in a social constructivist approach to researching children's experiences, each of which is taken up in more detail in the next several chapters.

Method	Advantages	Disadvantages
Participant observation	Observe cultural construction in action Observe interpersonal and context-individual dynamics Interpretation is continuous with data collection	Time consuming Role confusion
Interviews, individual	Focus on individual thought or experience Useful when topic may be sensitive or private, and its revelation could pose confidentiality or other ethical issues Supports individual point of view	Analysis often happens after the data are collected Child may try to give adult-friendly responses Question-and-answer mode of interaction may make children feel less powerful
Interviews, group	Focus is on interaction or collective knowledge Focus is on points of agreement and disagreement Individual contribution is enhanced by group Group experience may have empowering effect on disenfranchised individuals	Some may feel inhibited in a group Researcher perceived to be in a more powerful position Question-and-answer mode of interaction may make children feel less powerful Confidentiality issues
Informal interviews	Investigation of meaning and experience in context Flexibility and open ended Maintains least-adult role	Difficulty in recording data
Researcher-collected documents and artifacts • Formal text (policies, letters) • Informal text (notes) • Photographs • Video	Focus specifically on the researcher's interests In situ data that reflect the nature of interactions and communications in context	Significance may be different or unclear for participants
Participant-generated documents and artifacts • Photographs • Video • Drawings • Journals • Notes • Text messages	Children are in control of language and perspective Reflect natural modes of communication	Some are difficult to collect Some require special equipment and skills

FIGURE 4.1. Social constructivist methods for research with children.

DISCUSSION QUESTIONS

1. Describe the kind of relationship you hope to develop with your child participants. What personal attributes do you have that will help in the development of that relationship, and which ones potentially jeopardize aspects of that relationship? How do you expect your child participants to behave, and what behaviors do you know you will have difficulties with? What actions will you undertake to develop the kind of working relationship you hope for?

2. Find a research study where the researchers take a least-adult role in their work with children. Based on analysis of the study, what are the strengths and weaknesses of this approach? Describe reasons why you would adopt, alter, or reject such an approach in the study you hope to do with children.

3. How do you think child research participants would describe you? Consider your actions and interactions and the messages that might be embedded in them. Look for evidence of these messages in the responses the children demonstrate toward you. For example, who approaches you and talks to you openly? Who does not? What might this say about the role or style you have taken? Is there anything you might do differently to alter these dynamics?

CHAPTER 5

Ethical Challenges in Social Constructivist Research with Children

It is not only a question of seeing the world from children's perspectives but of acknowledging their rights to express their point of view or to remain silent.
—CLARK AND MOSS (2001, p. 7)

Treating children and young people as competent social actors rather than passive recipients of social norms creates new ethical challenges for researchers. Although research practices are guided by ethical codes and guidelines such as those described in the Belmont Report, these do not prevent ethical issues from arising during research, nor are these guidelines usually sufficient in determining an appropriate response. Furthermore, ethical issues arising in research with children are compounded by new conflicts of interest when children are treated by researchers as competent actors. Although permission to do research with children may be negotiated with adult gatekeepers, the interests of these same gatekeepers may conflict with those of children and researchers, and they may continue to regard children as vulnerable, dependent, inexperienced, or incompetent. Regardless of the particulars of a situation, children must be understood as having their own set of interests that may complement or oppose the interests of others (e.g., children, parents, teachers, researchers). Researchers working with children must be cognizant of the complex social situation in which child participants find themselves.

Ethical research with children requires that researchers adopt open communication with child participants (who may be unsure or confused about how to respond to being treated as competent social actors) and critical reflexivity toward all aspects of the research as it occurs (Alderson, 2004; Fraser, Lewis, Ding, Kellett, & Robinson, 2004). As discussed in Chapter 3, access is an ongoing process of which researchers should be aware. In this chapter, we reflect on the meaning and impact of conducting research with young people and the responsibilities and ethical issues that arise in the researcher–participant relationships that develop. Central to this discussion is the notion of voluntary participation; the ability to act or make a judgment based on one's own free choice. Considering young people's social status and power, is voluntary consent and participation feasible? If so, what does it take for children to understand and be able to exercise this choice?

VOLUNTARY PARTICIPATION

For the most part, children find themselves in situations where they are required to comply and do what adults ask of them. In school, teachers direct student activities, and any sense of choice or autonomy students do experience has been allowed by some adult or school authority. In clinical situations, children are asked to comply with interviews or examinations and are considered uncooperative if they refuse. On the street, children may gather and partake in children-led activities as long as they are not too noisy or behave in socially inappropriate ways. At home, children may have more choices but often have to ask permission of parents to go to the store or watch television. Therefore, when we talk about voluntary participation in research, children's social position makes their understanding of the notion of voluntariness complicated. Even when given the choice to comply or not to comply, different children likely understand that permission differently, as in this interaction between Kyle and Olivia, two suburban fourth graders who were working on a timeline of the high points and low points of what fourth grade was like for them:

RESEARCHER: I'm going to go over to the other group to see if they're finished. In the meantime, though, if you could draw a picture of your happiest memory in fourth grade someplace on here, wherever it happened and I'll be right back. (*Leaves.*)

KYLE: I hate drawing pictures. I can't draw pictures. I won't draw pictures.

OLIVIA: You have to. She said.

KYLE: I don't have to.

OLIVIA: Yes, you do.

KYLE: She said, "I'd like it if."

OLIVIA: Yup, so that means you should.

KYLE: She said, "I'd like it if you would." She didn't say, "Please go do it."

RESEARCHER: (*Returns to group and is asked by Kyle whether he has to draw.*) You don't have to.

KYLE: OK, because I can't draw pictures.

For Olivia the directions given by the researcher to draw a picture were taken as a requirement, whereas Kyle understood it as an option. When Kyle asks the researcher, he was given permission not to comply with her suggestion. In this situation, two groups of students had been working on separate timelines, and the researcher's suggestion to draw a picture of their happiest memory was offered to keep one group of children engaged while she checked the status of the other group.

Other situations are not so easily resolved, however. For example, we were pleased with how well our first focus group went with the urban fourth graders considering the diversity of the group. Even so, two of the 11 students had spoken little, and we were concerned about their lack of participation. English was not the girls' first language, and they simply nodded their responses or remained quiet during the open-ended discussion. However, when we ended the group by asking students to draw a picture of their teacher preparing them for the English Language Arts test, their depiction of their teacher along with a written description of the test preparation guidelines showed us they could share their experiences; they simply needed an approach that did not involve speaking. For our second focus group, therefore, we developed a writing activity that involved a typed question and space for students to write their answers. We were concerned that the students might balk at having to write and consider it too school-like, so we introduced it as a form of chain story where one student would have 3 minutes to respond and then they would have to pass their paper to the next student, who would then have 3 minutes to respond. As we began this activity, one student, Vincent, said he did not want to do it.

> RESEARCHER: We are going to write a little bit. Vincent, I need you to stay in your seat though, OK, because my recorder is not going to work if you keep shuffling around.
>
> VINCENT: I don't want to do it.
>
> RESEARCHER: (*ignoring Vincent and giving directions to the whole group*): We are going to give you a paper, some have pictures and some have questions, you are going to write for 3 minutes, we are going to time you, then we are going to tell you to pass it to the next person so it will be really quick, so try to write as much as you can about each of these things. (*Answers other students' questions.*)
>
> VINCENT: I don't want to write.
>
> RESEARCHER: That's OK. It's really fast. Just give it a try. What do you think? What happens? Go ahead and start.

We chose to incorporate writing and drawing activities in our range of data-collection tasks because it provided students who were uncomfortable speaking in a group an alternative outlet for expression. Not all students enjoyed all of the activities, and in most cases refusals to participate were acknowledged and alternative activities were provided. In the situation described previously, Vincent's repeated request not to write is not directly acknowledged. Although he could still decide to leave his responses blank, he was not actually given permission to withdraw from the activity. Whether right or wrong, our reason for not acknowledging his refusal that day occurred in the midst of other concerns. We had started the second group interview with these students with snacks and self-portraits and encouraged an atmosphere of relaxed small talk among the participants while they drew and ate. Different from our first meeting, we did not provide them with an overview of what we were going to do that day, wanting them to go into their self-portraits with few prompts or expectations. Most of the students responded to the lack of direction by happily talking among themselves. Some of the students, however, seemed more restless, and there was considerable wandering around the playroom. When we started the writing activity, we were aware of the way our meeting had taken on a "free time" feel and were concerned that some students might not want to start "work" again. Had Vincent walked away from the table or chosen not to write, we would have respected his choice. It was unclear, however, how openly giving him permission to withdraw from the activity would have affected the willingness of the other students to participate, especially the two other boys, Vincent's classmates and friends. It was in that context that Vincent's request was answered by encouraging him to "give it a try."

Group interviews present different challenges than individual interviews. In an individual situation, a child's reluctance to participate in an activity could be discussed and, if needed, an alternative provided. In a group situation, giving one student permission not to participate may affect how others choose to participate, and so the decision has to be made sensitively with the context and each participant's needs in mind. Davies (1982) argues that when children come to group situations, they bring with them whatever social relationships and issues formed in their day-to-day interactions with others in school or on the playground. In contrast, Nespor (1998) argues that the group interactions that occur in group interviews are "group-improvised performances" (p. 377) constructed by participants as they respond to the activities and dynamics of the research situation. We think it is a bit of both. Children come into group situations with expectations about what the group will involve and their own reputations, status, and dispositions. The researcher's introduction and the group activities will, in turn, provoke certain responses. Each meeting, therefore, is going to be a mixture of contextual and personal influences, some assisting rapport and the exchange of ideas, some impeding it. For example, one of the suburban eighth-grade students, prompted by our interest in the state tests, began asking research-like questions of her teachers. She would report to us her teachers' answers during subsequent meetings or in her journal. Her obvious interest in the process of inquiry affected her level of participation differently than students who were less interested. Similarly, in several of the groups, there was evidence of strong friendships, rivalry, and antagonism among participants. Depending on the study design, researchers have more or less time to get to know and understand the complexities of their participants' lives, which affects the nature of the interactions.

In our testing study, we met the fourth and eighth graders for three separate group interviews with no contact between group meetings. This made it more difficult to provide for good-quality rapport building. Nevertheless, having three meetings rather than one allowed students to develop a sense of who we were and what to expect during the meetings. We fostered a sense of fun; giving students whatever time they needed to complete tasks, following their leads whenever possible, and refraining from censoring, judging, or correcting their responses, even when their choice of words and behavior might have seemed inappropriate. However, we did set ground rules and remind students to respect each other if someone teased or laughed at another's response, and we did expect students to listen when others spoke and behave responsibly in the spaces we had borrowed for the groups. Adopting an attitude of "anything goes" we felt would be irresponsible and possibly frightening to children, who are used to having their behaviors monitored and controlled. We agree, however, with Nespor's (1998) assessment that children are not "interactional dopes emitting certain kinds of replies because . . . [he] asked questions a certain way" (p. 372). Children, like adults, however, do like to feel that they, and the researchers leading the activity, know what they are doing. Giving young people choices, therefore, needs to occur in a context where the reasons for and consequences of the choices have been discussed. In other words, developing ethical relationships is not a simple feat of guessing correctly about the needs and interests of children before meeting them, nor is it about adopting a *laissez-faire* attitude regarding children. Rather, it involves attention, listening well, flexibility, openness, asking for clarification, and providing space for questions and discussion, in other words an understanding that misunderstandings, new developments, new ideas, embarrassing moments, and false starts will occur. When working with children, attention to these situational factors and decisions about how to proceed come from adult researchers, who need to actively seek out assistance from child participants if their input is desired.

Christensen and Prout (2002) draw on various moral theories to argue that taking ethical responsibility *for* children is not equivalent to taking responsibility *away* from them. Children cannot be treated as a homogeneous group, nor can they be treated as being the same as adults. "Taking responsibility means entering a dialogue that recognizes commonality but also honours difference" (p. 480). They advocate a stance that they call "ethical symmetry," which takes as its starting point "the view that the ethical relationship between researcher and informant is the same whether he or she conducts research with adults or with children" (p. 482). Rather than presuming to understand children's interests and issues, this approach requires vigilance in attending to the personal characteristics of individuals as well as contextual factors, such as cultures of communication, language, and actions.

Developing ethical symmetry, or "empowering research relationships" (Holt, 2004), involves communication. Because children seem familiar with the terms researchers use, researchers can mistakenly assume that children also understand what they mean by those terms. Nespor (1998) described how the fourth and fifth graders he interviewed in an ethnographic study of school practices and culture began to question him about what he meant by "research." He found that the students associated the idea of research with "finding written knowledge already formulated in books or asking people to choose between well-defined options" (p. 375), a school-formulated notion of "doing research." Nespor goes on to describe how "doing research" was continuously redefined by his participants in the process of doing it. He concluded that because the meaning and practice of conducting research was embedded in the practice of doing it, a better approach would be to involve the participants as co-researchers as much as possible. In that way, children's understandings of school culture unfold through their research practices, a topic we take up in Chapter 10. What is important here is that children come to research relationships with some preconceptions of what "doing research" or "interviewing" or "drawing" means and that any data-collection technique is mediated by these understandings. It is important, therefore, that the practice and purpose of doing research become part of the conversation with participants alongside conversations about the research topic.

Ethical research involves having a regard and concern for the interests and needs of participants and those upon whom the findings of the research might have an impact. That is, doing research we have to be frank and critical about what, how and why our research is taking place . . . . We have to describe the circumstances in which an observation or measurement was made and who made the observation. (Fraser, 2004, p. 19)

COMMUNICATING RESPONSIBLY

Communicating responsibly is not that simple, however. David et al. (2001) describe how a seemingly straightforward process of wanting to impart an adequate amount of information about their study topic so that their potential participants could make an informed decision may have crossed the line from information providing to educating and even to propaganda. They wanted to interview children, ages 5 to 16 years, individually and in groups about their understanding of parental involvement. To do so, they gained access to several schools, ran classroom discussions about their project, created flyers to pass out to students and teachers, and had students complete a checklist about their interest in participating. Reflecting on their approach, they raise several questions about the process of informed consent that have implications for understanding the nature of communication with young people. First is the way communicating any information within a particular setting alters that communication, both how the information is received by potential participants and how it is delivered. Researchers, like David et al., may find themselves leading the class like a teacher might in a brainstorming session on the role of parents in schools. Second, written information like David et al.'s leaflets was meant to inform students but could be interpreted more radically as "signalling that children and young people could and should be questioning and challenging dominant received ideas about parental involvement in education" (p. 353). In contrast to the assumption of a "liberal approach to children and their rights to a voice" (p. 353), the researchers found themselves using bright colors and images that they (as adults with stereotypical views of childhood) thought would appeal to young people, thus reproducing commonly held conceptions of children. Finally, in trying to appeal to the children and seek their participation, David et al. describe a researcher-led process that resembled an advertising campaign, a process to sell a product to potential buyers.

As we seek ways to empower young people to make decisions for themselves, we do so within well-established institutionalized relationships that, for the most part, deny young people that same right. As such, our questions need to be considered within the research contexts we create with our participants and within these established frameworks. If children were merely recipients of institutional norms, the task would not be so difficult, but children are competent, interpreting beings who draw on multiple resources and promote a range of interests in their negotiations of different social situations. "If kids do not necessarily interpret researchers' queries, even peremptory ones, as teacher-like interrogations to be answered docilely, we need to rethink the methodological premise that roles and discourse forms are coupled in obligatory linkages" (Nespor, 1998, p. 373). In other words, researchers cannot rely on predetermined assumptions about how children will interpret the research situation or how characteristics like race, gender, and age will affect the research relationship before engaging with the participants themselves. These assumptions underestimate the active role children take in shaping the interaction. Children do use their previous experiences interacting with adults as a basis for negotiating the new interaction, but to suggest they simply respond as if the researcher is a teacher or parent misses the point. Children use the situation itself to form their interpretations of it and in doing so reveal a lot about how they understand that situation. For example, Nespor (1998) shares an interaction where he is explaining confidentiality to a group of students and tells the students that he will not share the information with parents or teachers. He goes on to say that, because he is only asking about schoolwork and nothing personal, the students need not be too concerned about confidentiality. Right after saying this, one of the students states, "Miss Flipper slapped me across the face" (p. 376).

> It took me a while to realize that comments like Lucy's might reveal more about the kids' perspectives on school than their answers to my questions about the writing process. It took me longer to realize that their comments revealed something of their understandings of the research process itself. The problem wasn't that they misread my work in terms of more familiar teacher-directed tasks, it was that from their standpoint the pragmatic uses of the activity were very different from

mine. If the kids sometimes acted as though I had no power over them, ignoring my questions or making fun of them, they seemed at the same time to think I had some power over their teachers. (Nespor, 1998, p. 376)

Whether Nespor's assessment of the students' intention is correct or not, child participants may not always interpret the research situation in the same way the adult researchers do, and even if they do, they may choose another purpose as well. Children do not automatically view the research interaction as research oriented, meaning as being primarily about an exchange or construction of information about a topic of which they have knowledge. Rather, a closer focus on how young people understand the research interaction can strengthen an understanding or interpretation of the data that are collected in these interactions. It is important to reflect on the possible ways children are making sense of and manipulating the research situation to meet their own needs.

Despite young people's agency and their ability to manipulate the research situation, it is necessary to remind ourselves of their social positions in society. The ability to manipulate a social situation or express one's desires and needs does not necessarily support the presence of voluntariness. In fact, the belief in one's lack of voluntariness can play a role in how young people make sense of and use the research process. For example, young people make use of the research relationship to share troubles they are having at home or in school, such as the example provided by Nespor. Researchers may assume this kind of interaction signals a lack of opportunities for young people to share personal issues with attentive and caring adults. Although the benefits of these personal relationships are important to nurture, it is also important to keep an open mind about other ways young people are exploiting and benefiting from the research relationship. For example, when Nespor (1998) turned over research decisions to a group of fourth graders, he found that the children's primary interest was gathering children's voices to make a case against some feature of their school lives that they wanted changed, such as a homework policy. This suggests that children actively interpret social situations such as research relationships and find ways to get the most out of them in response not only to what the research situation offers but to the constraints and opportunities of their daily lives as well. In the Nespor example, one could argue the students used the research to gather students' voices and saw this as an opportunity to legitimately use that voice to effect change, perhaps because the lack of power to do so is a feature of their student life.

Inviting young people to become participants in research studies, therefore, can create bridges between several social situations, each with their respective norms and rules of conduct. In some situations, as in the example just described, the bridging creates opportunities for children to infiltrate and affect the systems they live with. In other situations, such as when researchers ask young people to talk about themselves, their parents, teachers, or friends, young people are asked to take on more of an informant role, which requires a complex set of social negotiations and understandings. Young participants are aware of social norms about sharing private information and can find themselves uncertain about what to say about certain people: What is the researcher really seeking to know about X? Is it OK to share this about X? Would X be angry if I shared this? It is not always possible or easy to determine the impact of researchers' questions on participants' personal senses of selves. For example, we noticed that some students seemed uncomfortable talking about how their parents interacted with them around school activities, a space where private home and public school meet. It is also asking them to share a personal self with a group of peers with whom they may have only shared a public self. On the other hand, it was not uncommon for participants to help each other give a "fair" picture of someone they knew in common. For example, when talking about a teacher, students often stepped in to add to a story someone had shared or balance a statement if he or she felt the other student had exaggerated. Thus, although group work can potentially enrich responses by developing a shared story over time, it can also prevent the development of themes and topics less comfortably discussed in a public forum. The point is that the way participants understand what they can and cannot reveal in an interview interaction mixes personal and social experiences and will not be the same for any two participants. Young people's social position does make them more vulnerable to pressure from researchers and to misunderstanding the range of their rights to participate or to withdraw or remain silent. Communicating responsibly needs to balance all of these factors simultaneously. It requires empathy, vigilance, and an awareness of possible motives and interests. And it requires keeping the children's interests in the forefront.

So what does communicating responsibly look like? It means

- ■ Going beyond answering students' questions to anticipating these questions.

- ■ Relying on our social sensitivities and intuitions as we relate to different children rather than on predetermined assumptions about age, race, gender, disability, and other socially constructed characteristics.

- ■ Openly discussing with our participants the desired processes and outcomes of our work and what we hope to gain from engaging them in the planned research activities.

- ■ Finally, reflecting on our behaviors and learning from our participants so that we can develop more ethical and responsible approaches in future work.

The need for such reflection was made evident to us during the final meeting with the urban fourth graders. Although the children in the suburban and eighth-grade groups seemed to view our meetings as extracurricular events and to understand that these would occur three times and then end, it was unclear how much the urban fourth graders understood about the nature of this relationship. As we walked into the school to gather the urban fourth graders for their third meeting with us, it was obvious that the entire school was in turmoil. In the entryway to the principal's office were five students (one, Savannah, who was part of our group) waiting to face what seemed to be serious disciplinary charges. One boy was kicking the principal, two girls (including Savannah) were being sent home, and two boys were facing possible criminal charges for having destroyed property (at least that is what the secretary was telling them) and were cowering under their chairs. The principal was not interested in letting Savannah come to our research group, and we saw her leaving in his car as we went to gather the other children. The remaining 10 students were scattered in different classrooms, but the three boys all came from the same one. As I (Freeman) peeked through the classroom door, the atmosphere made me hesitate to knock. It was dark, and the students all had their heads bent over a packet of work. When the teacher was reminded who was in our research study (Vincent, Jake, and Joseph), she was obviously unhappy and informed me that these were the three who were bad in music. The boys retorted that it was not them. I told them that I was happy to see them and asked if they still wanted to meet with me. As the boys followed me out the door, the teacher told them that they would have to finish the packet for homework then. The boys already upset were now very upset and informed me that they would throw the homework out and that it was unfair that they had to do it. We started the group with snacks to allow the children to talk about what happened that day. And the children vented, not just about school and teachers, but about us as well. We listened and empathized with the students' anger, and then Jake suddenly turned his attention toward one of us:

JAKE: How long have we been here?

RESEARCHER: You mean, like here today?

JAKE: No. How long have we been here with you?

RESEARCHER: The first time we met was in January.

JAKE: So, like, May . . .

RESEARCHER: What, 5 months?

JAKE: Yeah. I hoped you were coming because I had the feeling you were coming.

JOSEPH: This is the last time?

RESEARCHER: Yeah.

JOSEPH: (*anger in his voice*) Then why was it so long?

RESEARCHER: Between last time and this time?

JOSEPH: Yeah. Why every time you come here it's like a long time?

While Jake wanted us to know that he valued our times together and possibly thought about us coming in between sessions, Joseph's comment reveals a serious breach in communication. Scheduling group meetings and finding a time that worked for all students as well as the teachers (since we were meeting during school hours) was complicated. However, we could have done a better job of keeping the participants informed of our planned comings and goings. A calendar depicting the months of the year and the probable dates of our meetings as well as a quick note the day before would have given the children a better sense of control over these events. Not doing so was disrespectful and disempowering. In a world where grown-ups expect certain things from students, what can they expect from us? We know we showed the students care and respect, and we offered them a variety of opportunities to express their perspectives and opinions on different topics, some of which mattered to them, some of which did not. However, for some students, like some of the urban students, it was probable that we not only fell short of their expectations, but the vagueness of our role in their lives may have left them with feelings of uncertainty and disappointment.

Even while researchers tell young participants that their participation is voluntary, it is important to reflect on how our behavior tells a different story. The fact that we control the dates and times of our meetings and decide on the questions to ask and activities to do gives priority to our agenda. When one participant fails or refuses to answer a question, the fact that we turn to another for an answer establishes an expectation that the question is right and the answer is desired. These may be realities of the research relationship, but they reinforce to young people the reality of their lives, which is usually predetermined for them and non-negotiable. If we are to use the opportunities present in research relationships to empower children, then we need to think more broadly and more carefully about all aspects of this relationship.

RECIPROCITY

One way to think about keeping the children's interests in the forefront is to emphasize the notion of reciprocity. What can participating in a research study offer child participants? As we have suggested throughout this book, participatory techniques such as giving children choices throughout the study can help establish ethical and empowering relationships. There are, of course, different levels of involvement, and children can become co-researchers in their own right, as we see in Chapter 10. Most of the time, however, children are invited as participants in researcher-led research projects. In these situations, reciprocity can take different shapes, but its emphasis can help establish empowering relationships between participants and researchers. "The researcher's desire to gain information from child participants without giving something in return reflects an underlying sense of the adult researcher's privilege. However, by giving something in return for receiving this information, researchers can reduce the potential power inequality" (Eder & Fingerson, 2003, p. 37).

The students in our study expressed different reasons for feeling positive about their participation. The eighth graders liked receiving the movie tickets and gift certificates for their participation, were interested in what their peers had to say, and felt good about their ability to contribute to our understanding of how students experience state testing. The fourth graders liked the movie tickets, the snacks, the games, the drawings, using the tape recorders, and spending time with us. Understanding what young people get out of these research relationships is crucial to understanding how to foster more meaningful and reciprocal relationships.

Just having someone to talk to can be meaningful and empowering to young people. Understanding how to communicate openly with young people about research goals and practices and the essential contributions participants make to developing social understandings is important. So is, however, recognizing our participants' contributions openly by providing compensation for their time. Social science research routinely compensates adults for their participation in research, often with cash, and researchers should expect to provide appropriate compensation to children and youth for their participation. Finding the right kind and amount of compensation (money, gift cards, movie passes, iTunes cards, books, pizza parties) is dependent on the age of the children, the context, and whether the participation is individual or as a group.

Reciprocity can also mean giving something back to the community. As in Nespor's study, children may use the research process to work for change that immediately and directly affects their lives. This is one sense of giving something back to the community. However, there is a broader sense as well, a sense of doing research that contributes to the well-being of children and youth beyond those in a particular research study. Communicating with policymakers and politicians, social activism (organizing, lobbying, demonstrating), giving legal testimony, and promoting youth-led participatory research are some forms of this kind of reciprocity.

Reciprocity does not resolve unequal and disempowering relationships; it becomes part of the ongoing search for responsible communication and ethical practice. Hearing what students have to say, observing their responses to research activities and questions, and experiencing their closeness and trust as well as their distance and suspicions help researchers not only to see and understand better what students are capable of but also to understand the effect of research as a social practice. Awareness, openness, flexibility, and patience are all necessary, but a belief in the intelligence, worth, and capability of each student is a must when working with children. Although the ethical challenges remain complex, the rewards go beyond the information gathered: in the privilege we have as researchers to engage with and learn from the lives and voices of children and youth.

DISCUSSION QUESTIONS

1. In "'It's That Linda Again': Ethical, Practical, and Political Issues Involved in Longitudinal Research with Young Men," Linda McDowell (2001) undertook a multiple-interview study of working-class adolescent boys who were failing in school and facing a life of low-paying jobs or unemployment. Wanting to get their story "right," she viewed their reading of her interpretations of their lives as important. She was faced, however, with what she felt was an ethical dilemma because her descriptions of their lives and her determination of their future opportunities was bleak. She did not feel that sending them her written academic papers was appropriate and considered other possible approaches. What ethical issues are raised by sending, or not sending, the written work to these participants? What are some other ways that McDowell could share the results with the youth to get their feedback?

2. In "Intervening in Friendship Exclusion: The Politics of Doing Feminist Research with Teenage Girls," Kathryn Morris-Roberts (2001) is faced with an ethical dilemma in a year-long participant observation of girls' friendship groups. Hanging out with some groups necessarily involved excluding other groups, a reality that Morris-Roberts solved by openly moving from group to group. However, this did not prevent the group she was currently involved in to participate in behaviors that were oppressive, hurtful, or exclusionary to others (sometimes

to others who Morris-Roberts hung out with at other times). Believing that her feminist ideologies encouraged her to challenge injustice when she saw it happening did not prevent Morris-Roberts from inadvertently participating in those oppressive behaviors. For example, she found herself including only some girls for a photography project; a fourth girl was told there were not enough cameras when it was obvious the other three did not want her in the project. What steps could Morris-Roberts have taken to communicate her moral position more openly to her participants, and how do you think doing so would have altered her relations with her participants? Discuss the issue with a classmate and come up with a solution to the photography project that would have been more inclusive of all who wanted to participate. Brainstorm some general strategies that you could use in situations where you are a witness to oppressive or exclusionary behaviors.

CHAPTER 6

Interviewing

The interview elicits interpretations of the world, for it is itself an object of interpretation. But the interview is not an interpretation of the world per se. Rather it stands in an interpretive relationship to the world that it creates.
—DENZIN (2001, p. 30)

Interviewing may be the most ubiquitous data-collection strategy in the social sciences. Indeed, Holstein and Gubrium (1995) estimate that nearly 90% of social science research includes the collection of interview data. Denzin (2001) suggests that we have become an interview society, one in which the interview form is a primary way of interacting in many social contexts (e.g., giving a medical history) and a mode of interaction depicted in both print and nonprint media. Adults and children alike are exposed to the interview form as part of their cultural knowledge, and so it is little wonder that interviews are favored by social scientists.

Research interviewing can take different forms, from informal conversations occurring over time within participant observation studies to more semistructured interactions requiring a separate time and space. Unlike participant observation approaches, which generally allow young participants to take the lead in determining the nature of the activity or topic of conversation, interviewing, by its very structure, is usually planned by the researcher. As we discuss in this chapter, this does not preclude opportunities for participants to direct the conversation, only that in general an interview provides a space to talk about something that has been determined in advance.

Interviewing children, whether individually or in groups, is rewarding work. Interviews reveal story fragments, narrative representations of social experiences, and the meanings they might have to the speaker. With planning, attention to details, flexibility of design, and the belief that children and adolescents are worth listening to, the likelihood is that the interview will go well, perhaps not as planned and not with the expected results but nonetheless a positive experience. Within a social constructivist framework, the individual or group interview is viewed as a social event that enables children to express their interpretations of events and experiences within the interview interaction. Individual interviews provide a personal space for children or adolescents to voice their thoughts on an issue, share an experience, or reflect on an event. The focus is on the individual child in relation to a particular topic and on the child–adult interaction. Group interviews diffuse the attention of the researcher across all participants as well as provide a setting for children to interact with peers on common topics. In our study of student experiences with state-mandated testing in schools, eighth-grade participants expressed appreciation for the opportunity to hear what their classmates had to say about testing and test preparation. Interviewing children in groups may also reduce the researcher's power within the research context, because the presence of peers will typically take precedence over the presence of the researcher.

Figure 6.1 illustrates that 9-year-olds are quite capable of sitting in a group, listening to the researcher's questions and peers' responses, and sharing their own experiences. The fact that they can do it does not mean that they always will or that facilitating such interactions is a straightforward affair. This group interview occurred after we divided 12 student participants into two groups, provided time for children to draw self-portraits of themselves taking the test, and listened to each describe their feelings during the test and how they represented that feeling in the drawing. Once in small groups, the researcher used a role-playing approach suggesting she was a newspaper reporter who was interested in how each student represented him- or herself in their drawings. This approach worked well, even though one group dissolved into uncontrolled giggles because one of

RESEARCHER: What was the most important strategy that you used on the [English Language Arts test]?

KYLE: On the first time when we were doing the fill in the bubble, probably the most important strategy was to read the questions and then to go back and read the story.

RESEARCHER: OK, so you read the questions first and then you went back.

KYLE: Yeah, on the first day.

ANDREW: The most important strategy that I used, or it's not important, but I went and asked the teacher if I can read it to her, and then it made sense again after I read it to her [MEGAN: Yeah!], because sometimes you miss on a word and then you don't know what it is, but it doesn't make sense, and then you go and tell the teacher "I don't get it," and then she usually has you read it to her, and it makes sense.

RESEARCHER: So reading it out loud helps you.

ANDREW: Yes.

MEGAN: I never thought of doing that but I like that idea.

RESEARCHER: Did you have a most important strategy?

MORGAN: My most important strategy is to read, I mean, is to read through the questions first, and then you read them twice, or if you want you read it one time, and then you can read the story. So it takes less time, and if you find the answer in the book you can, you can just fill what you have to write about that.

MEGAN: Um, when I do, like the ones where you have to answer a question with writing, um, I go through and first I read the question and then I write a sentence starter for most of them, and then I go on and keep going until I'm at the end of it, and then from the beginning I read it and I fill it in, and if I can't figure it out then I skip that again, and I go on to other ones. So I have the hardest one for last, but I can sit and concentrate on it more because there are only one or two, instead of if I spent all my time on that then the rest of the questions would be unanswered.

FIGURE 6.1. Excerpt from a group interview with fourth-grade suburban students.

the boys made silly faces to the student being "interviewed" behind the back of the researcher acting as a reporter.

This chapter discusses the strengths and weaknesses of individual and group interviewing and then presents a variety of strategies to elicit interview responses from children in ways that are engaging and open-ended and that feel safe. As we discussed in Chapter 4, consideration must be given to the researcher–participant relationship, the setting where the research or interview is to be conducted, and the reason for using interviews.

INTERVIEWING AS A RELATIONSHIP

From a social constructivist perspective, interviewing is a relationship in which the researcher and participant collaborate to construct a narrative, a storytelling experience that orders some experiences and understandings of the material world. An interview cannot be seen as "an expression of the interviewee's own 'authentic voice'" (Alldred & Burman, 2005, p. 181); it is not a revelation of the true private self. Nor is it a reflection of some external world. Indeed, there are no true private selves nor single external worlds to be revealed, only contextual presentations of meaning and experience. The interview itself is a co-constructed narrative of meaning and experience. In Figure 6.1, the experiences of the researcher are reflected in the questions asked, in this case about what sorts of strategies kids used while taking the test. The story of these kids' strategic engagement in the testing event is coauthored by the researcher and all of the children involved in the interview.

All interviews require that participants determine, among other things, the purpose of the interview, their relationship with the interviewers, how they will negotiate the presence of peers in group situations, the meaning of specific questions, the directions to different activities, and the spoken and unspoken rules of engagement of this social event. Differences in contexts, interviewers, topics, time of day, and age of participants all need to be taken into account when seeking to establish an interviewer–interviewee relationship that will produce high-quality data on the topic of interest. It is important to remember that the interview is not an everyday interaction, and so socialization into ways of being and behaving in the interview is often necessary, especially with children who are likely to define it by relating it to other similar activities with teachers and professionals.

When care is taken to explain the research project in ways that children understand, there is every reason to believe they are capable of making a decision about whether or not they wish to be interviewed. Depending on the interview topic, however, it may also be important to clarify for children what actions, such as changes to their living situation or health condition, can and cannot happen as a result of the interview. It is important to be clear about what this encounter entails, especially for children involved in similar-appearing relationships with tutors, therapists, case workers, or counselors. In these cases, interview interactions may be meant expressly to identify problems and possibilities for amelioration, but seldom is this taken for granted in a research interview. So the limits of a research interview need to be clear.

An interview's effectiveness resides in the closeness and intimacy of the interaction between researcher and participants as well as its purposefulness. Participants are invited to talk about *something*. The personal nature of the interaction gives the researcher flexibility to seek more information, probe for more detail, or "follow up on vague, confusing, even contradictory information, sensitively and systematically" (Rogers, Casey, Ekert, & Holland, 2005, p. 159). It also gives freedom to interview participants to answer in their own way, using their own terms, and making their own connections to the interview topic. Children and youth have an opportunity to use their own language and voice rather than employing adult language and interpretations. "The central challenge before the researcher who uses the interview is the *management* of the relationship so it facilitates but does not contaminate the collection of subjective data" (Parker, 1984, p. 19). Therefore, researchers must not only choreograph but must monitor and acknowledge the role they play in interviews with participants.

Competencies of Children and Interviewers

In his commentary on what we know about young children's language competencies, Coles (1996) provides two examples of how our questions reflect our views about language and meaning. When language is viewed as the means by which people communicate what they mean and know, then our questions are seen as a tool to get at that knowledge, much like "teacher questions which often demand quick, terse, factual answers and leave little time for children to respond, elaborate or reason out loud" (p. 13). But when language and meaning are interconnected and shape each other, then our "questions have a particular potency since their role is to help realize thought which is yet unthought, which is only potential" (p. 14). A social constructivist interview engagement is of the latter sort, an opportunity to co-construct meaning.

Although much has been written about children's competencies as interviewees, these competencies are a function of the mutual abilities of the interviewer and interviewee to relate and communicate with each other. The many studies that have now been conducted with children show that, even at a very young age, children have the capacity to be participants in research, to understand what is being asked of them, and to share their experiences in response (Clark, 2004). Different children, whether because of age, inexperience, language ability, or attention span, will promote different forms of interaction. It is important, however, not to predefine those differences too narrowly but rather approach each child or group of children as responding to a situation that may be unfamiliar, so that an otherwise articulate child may become quite mute or a tense, serious child may become silly.

Responding to every individual as a person-in-situation (Westcott & Littleton, 2005, p. 147) can enable the researcher to respond sensitively and appropriately to a variety of behaviors. In our focus groups with fourth and eighth graders, for example, we found that participants whose first language was not English were reluctant to speak aloud in the group. Their silence could have been construed as shyness or inability to understand the question. When we asked similar questions in writing, we found they understood our questions and were able to respond in writing. Had we assumed simply that they could not understand, we might not have provided them with an alternative way of responding.

> Rather than theorizing incompetence . . . we need to develop our understanding of the activity and responses of the child in context. We need to understand how the situations in which children are placed, and the meanings they ascribe to interviewer's questions, support or constrain their activity and performance. We also need to recognize that notions of "competence" are problematic, and are informed by cultural beliefs and negotiated by participants in particular social, institutional and cultural contexts. (Westcott & Littleton, 2005, p. 146)

This requires attention to the child as a meaning-making, active agent, which poses a challenge to researchers who do not inhabit the same cultural space or social position as children and young people. Figure 6.2 summarizes characteristics of a good interviewer of children and youth.

- Develops rapport with youth.
- Genuinely demonstrates empathy with youth.
- Calms an anxious, shy, or hostile young person.
- Invites and responds to youth questions and concerns during the interview.
- Allows youth to participate in setting the direction of and strategies within the interview.
- Clearly communicates the purpose of the interview.
- Uses appropriate language and sentence structure.
- Asks open-ended questions and follow-up questions to encourage youth to tell their story.
- Gets an interview back on track when a young person becomes fixated on one question or responds in a silly way.

FIGURE 6.2. Characteristics of a good interviewer of children and youth.

DEVELOPING INTERVIEW QUESTIONS AND PROTOCOLS

Questions and answers are forms of communication that consist of two primary features: "They contain both *informational* and *relational* intentions" (Tammivaara & Enright, 1986, p. 219, emphasis in original). The informational refers to the *what* of that which is being communicated and the relational to *how* the information is understood within the relational context of the interaction, but neither stands alone. Besides the relational challenges already discussed in Chapter 4, different questions will shape the interaction in different ways. Drawing from Lortie's (1975) work, Tammivaara and Enright suggest four dimensions for developing questions: direct–indirect, abstract–concrete, personal–impersonal, and cathected–low affect (p. 222).

Although Lortie studied teachers' goals and perspectives on teaching, his views on the nature of questions and their relation to data elicitation are more broadly relevant. Lortie discussed three types of questions and their usefulness for understanding the core of teachers' experiences: (1) direct and personal, (2) indirect and concrete, and (3) indirect, personal, concrete, and cathected (i.e., connected to emotions), which he felt to be most valuable. In our work with fourth- and eighth-grade students, an example of a direct and personal question might be, "What do you do when you feel nervous while you are taking a state test? How did you learn that?" An

indirect, concrete question might be, "How does your teacher let you
know what he or she expects during the ELA [English Language
Arts test]?" Indirect, personal, concrete, and cathected questions
might be, "What do you think happens to students who don't pass
the state tests? Who do you think is responsible for their failure?"
Having more than one kind of question provides multiple opportunities for children to narrate their experiences and the meaning
they ascribe to them.

Within a social constructivist interview, it is necessary for the
researcher to create and maintain a nonjudgmental response. Communicating a dislike for or discomfort with some responses (such as
the use of curse words or racist comments) will either end the interview or result in the co-creation of a narrative of youth experience
driven by a particular moralism. We experienced a slightly different
manifestation of this when an interview with a group of inner-city
teens was interrupted by the personnel running the after-school
program in which the youth were participating. Program staff were
reluctant to allow us to interview the youth without their presence,
because they perceived we were likely incapable of handling situations that might arise. During the interview, several youth played
out some long-standing and personal disagreements, which resulted
in shouting and aggressive physical posturing. As interviewers, the
relationships among the youth helped to understand how they
understood themselves within this program, but the noisy exchange
resulted in the program staff bursting into the interview and bringing it to a halt. Our nonjudgmental response to the youth increased
our credibility with the youth but diminished our credibility with the
program staff.

It is a common mistake to develop interview protocols that are
too broad or too abstract. For example, one might ask, "What moti-
vates you to learn?" or "What role do you see yourself playing among
your friends?" Such a question begs other questions: What is motivation, what is role, what do they look like, and what are you really
trying to understand about these concepts? For example, role can be
understood as the quality of a person's presence in a particular setting; an alternative question might be, "If you suddenly had to go live
with your uncle for a month, what would your friends miss most about
you? What would they have to do to fill the gap you left? Who would
be most affected? Why? How?" Understanding as much as possible
what is relevant about role or motivation within the research context allows the researcher to empathize with the other and thus ask

questions that elicit rich stories about their experiences. This is especially important with children because many of the words we take
for granted are abstract, and so rethinking abstract terms in relation
to children's daily experience is important. Open-ended questions
are almost always better. "If the questions are open-ended, the children will have more opportunity to bring in the topics and modes
of discourse that are familiar to them. Also, nondirected questions
provide more opportunity for children in group interviews to collaborate in their answers and to expand on the responses of others"
(Eder & Fingerson, 2003, p. 36).

More important perhaps than the kinds of questions is the interview structure. The interview is an interaction between or among
people who typically do not know each other. Paying attention to the
setting, initial greetings, opening activity, subsequent activities, and
closing comments are all essential components to a successful interview situation. If child participants do not feel welcome immediately,
they may ask to leave. Consider the context. How comfortable and
welcoming is the designated interview space? How will you and your
participants be seated? Take the time to find an informal, friendly
place, or make a formal space more inviting by bringing in a few
props (cushions, stuffed animals, markers, and paper) and equally
sized chairs or a rug to sit on. Consider the time of day, avoiding
scheduling conflicts such as a child's favorite TV show. Consider the
importance of using an icebreaker or warm-up activity.

Interviews often begin with open-ended questions to allow the
child to become comfortable talking to you before engaging with the
topic of interest. However, with children, especially younger ones,
it is essential to capture their attention even before you begin the
questions. Icebreakers work well. If this is an individual interview, a
drawing game like Winnicott's (1971) squiggle game works well: The
researcher makes a squiggle on a piece of paper and then asks the
child to turn it into something. Once done, the child makes a squiggle
for the researcher to turn into something. In a group situation, the
choice of icebreaker should help group members get to know each
other and promote group cohesiveness. Games, such as lining up
according to month of birth, throwing a ball around and stating your
name, or a favorite activity or music group, work with a wide range of
age groups. Using visuals or other elicitation strategies should not be
reserved for icebreakers and can be important strategies for generating responses. "Young children generally find *doing* something *with*
something and talking *about* that something to be easier, more com-

fortable, and more interesting than only talking about something that isn't physically present" (Tammivaara & Enright, 1986, p. 232). "To focus solely on discourse processes neglects a further important sense in which meaning is created—namely, through our engagement with, and use of, tools and artifacts" (Tammivaara & Enright, 1986, pp. 147–148). Figure 6.3 provides tips for successful interviews with children and youth.

Before
- Develop complete protocol with backup activities for shy or hesitant participants.
- Consider alternative activities such as drawing, writing, keeping a written or audio journal, taking pictures, or using video clips, pictures, scenarios, maps, or other visual elicitation strategies to engage the children.
- When planning for drawing or other creative activities, consider what you want to be able to do with these products in the future and plan to use darker markers and paper sizes that are manageable.
- Check out the room where the interview is to be conducted.
- Set up recording equipment before children arrive.

During
- Address children by name.
- Remind children of the purpose for the interview and let them know how it will be structured.
- Ask open-ended questions.
- Use clear, explicit language for directions and questions.
- Let children take the lead in the process whenever possible.
- Express empathy authentically.
- Treat children with respect, but remember that child and adolescent behavior is unpredictable.
- Place recorders on a notebook rather than right on the table.
- If providing snacks, stay away from noisy packaging.

After
- Assign pseudonyms and label all tapes, drawings, and other materials.
- Transcribe interviews immediately and record important information about the interview such as the children's and researcher's attitude, behavior, receptivity, and other pertinent information such as interruptions.
- Revise the protocol if necessary.

FIGURE 6.3. Tips for interviewing children and adolescents.

STRATEGIES FOR ELICITING VERBAL RESPONSES

Interviews with children work best when structured around several activities (Graue & Walsh, 1998; Mauthner, 1997). This breaks the routine and helps children stay engaged; each activity can mark a new focal point or be a different way of asking similar questions. Having something specific to respond to helps younger children make connections to the topic of inquiry.

> For example, pictures of the children in a classroom can be very useful for getting at children's understandings of classroom social interactions. One might array the photos on a table, then pick out the photo of Mary and ask, "If Mary was working at the art table, what other children would come and work with her?" (Graue & Walsh, 1998, pp. 114–115)

The use of prompts when interviewing children is not new. Child therapists and clinicians working with children have been using them for years. Dolls, toys, and puppets have been used to elicit information about suspected child abuse, to allow children to act out their feelings, or to tell a story (Brooker, 2001). More recently, researchers have turned to a variety of elicitation props so children and young people are able to share everyday experiences. Finding ways to tap into the lived experiences of children, researchers have invited children to

- Role-play scenarios concerning living with asthma (M. Morgan et al., 2002).
- Create and act out dramatic scenes of real-life issues (Veale, 2005).
- Watch and respond to short video clips from television programs "as a springboard for further discussion about how young people cope with their problems and how they perceive adults' reactions to their problems" (Punch, 2002a, p. 51).
- Use blueprints of the interior of their school to identify violent events that had occurred in the past year and then use these as the basis for a focus group discussion with peers (Astor, Meyer, & Behre, 1999).
- Fill out a "pocket decision-maker chart" representing significant decisions they had made in their life and the people who contributed to them (Thomas & O'Kane, 1998).

We have constructed interview questions as beginnings of sentences that children would choose out of a hat, read out loud, and then complete. We call it the Honesty Game because, as we told the students, the intention is that you finish the question as honestly as you can. Although this game functioned much like any open-ended question, the act of selecting a question from a hat and having something to hold in one's hand prompted students to respond, whereas they may not have responded to a spoken question. It allowed students not to have to memorize the question, and they enjoyed passing around the tape recorder and speaking into it. When we first used this strategy, the students suggested that more than one student could finish each sentence beginning, a strategy we readily incorporated because it allowed children a significant role in defining the interview situation and because it gave us fuller, more complex data. We also used the interaction to probe other topics if the opportunity arose, such as in this example of a group interview with urban fourth graders:

> JAKE: *The kids who fail the ELA* . . . have to repeat the grade.
>
> TRACY: *The kids who fail the ELA* . . . didn't pay attention and didn't do what they were supposed to do.
>
> DAPHNE: *The kids who fail the ELA* . . . didn't think about the tricks that the teacher had taught them.
>
> RESEARCHER: Can you think of one of those tricks?
>
> [The children introduced us to the notion of trickery, both in terms of attempts by the test makers to trick them and in terms of the tricks the kids used to do well on the test.]
>
> DAPHNE: You have to read the question very, very carefully.
>
> ALEXA: If you see an answer that you might think is right, still go back and read the other answers.
>
> FAITH: Answer the question very, very carefully.

Stimulus Drawing Approaches

Images have long been used to elicit responses in therapeutic consultations and in art therapy. The well-known Rorschach inkblot test is based on the assumption that people's immediate free associations can open a path into their emotional or subconscious worlds. These tests, known as "stimulus tests," evolved into combinations of stimuli and responses, creating a more interactive give-and-take between therapist and patient, especially when working with children. For example, the Draw a Story test starts off with 14 stimulus cards depicting a variety of situations. The child is asked to select two pictures and then draw and narrate a story based on the subject of those two pictures. The emotional content of the responses is then rated using a predetermined scale. "In the stimulus drawing approach, drawing takes the place of words as the principal channel for receiving and expressing ideas" (Silver, 2001, p. 16).

As we discuss in Chapter 7, the use of drawing in social science research typically involves participant-produced drawings. Although stimulus methods such as Silver's are still widely used when working with children, especially in the fields of psychology and social work, those methods are not the ones advocated in this book. A social constructivist approach views images as a visual resource that assists in the co-construction of understanding and meaning on a topic of interest. As researchers consider the options available, it is not uncommon to see them using drawings to tap into the emotional and cognitive lives of children, a stimulus sorting task to understand children's perceptions or relations to certain people or activities, written tasks for information on specific events, and open-ended interview questions for understanding children's experiences.

Photoelicitation Interviewing

Using photographs is one such elicitation strategy. Photoelicitation is a way to not simply get more information but to evoke "a different kind of information" (Harper, 2002, p. 13). American photographer John Collier, Jr. (1913–1992) used photographs in interviews in the 1950s when he worked with a Cornell University research team examining mental health in changing Canadian communities. Collier (1957) noted that graphic imagery had a "compelling effect upon the informant, [with] its ability to prod latent memory, to stimulate and release emotional statements about the informant's life" (p. 858). Using photographs in interviews with children is helpful to build rapport and to disrupt children's preset ideas about one-on-one interactions with adults (Cappello, 2005; Dempsey & Tucker, 1994; Mauthner, 1997) or, in Collier's terms, "shatter the composure of a guarded reply" (1957, p. 854). Photoelicitation is effective with children and has been used in a variety of contexts and for a variety of purposes: to explore 5- to 13-year-olds' attitudes and beliefs about different careers (Weiniger, 1998); thoughts about disabilities (Diamond, 1996); differences in historical thinking in third-, sixth-, and ninth-grade children (Foster, Hoge, & Rosch, 1999); and the effects of magazine images of beauty on 14- to 18-year-old female athletes' physical self-concept (Hurworth, Clark, Martin, & Thomsen, 2005).

Using photoelicitation requires the selection of images with the research goal in mind, some idea of its relevance or import to the respective participants, and an understanding of its purpose within the larger research design (i.e., to expand on themes the researcher has identified as potentially significant, to build rapport and explore participant-expressed ideas in the beginning of a new interview, to elicit a group response on a topic around a shared image).

In her investigation of writing practices with young children in an urban southern California elementary school, Cappello (2005) conducted individual photoelicitation interviews with 6- to 9-year-old students. She observed the children in their classroom for several months, engaged them in formal and informal interviews, and invited them to take pictures of what they considered to be "important writing" at school using cameras they could sign out whenever they wanted. She was interested in how writing played a role in shaping the children's social identities and the kinds of decisions children made about their writing. When she prepared for each photo-driven interview, she focused on that child and his or her own photographs.

> The pictures in the kit included the likenesses of the participants engaged in the many stages of classroom writing . . . . The pictures were assembled in a large binder and protected by clear sleeves so the children could easily remove and organize them. Nearly a hundred 4 × 6 images were included in the kit. All were coded and numbered for easy refilling after the interview. The photographs were not captioned, but the binder was separated into three clearly defined sections: children at work, public displays, and informant-made images. (Cappello, 2005, p. 174)

In this example, the students did not see their own pictures before the interview and did not participate in the selection process. Instead, Cappello started off each interview by highlighting the images taken by the students themselves and using these as a basis for separating nonimportant from important images and then talking about them.

Researchers have used images in a variety of ways in their work with children, but only recently has the focus been on how the child or young person is using the medium to communicate and express a viewpoint within a specific interaction, not as an "objective" representation of some aspect of development or identity. In Chapter 7, we explore how researchers can incorporate art and photography in research with children.

INDIVIDUAL INTERVIEWS

Individual interviews prioritize the individual. Their strength is that they allow the researcher to give each participant his or her complete attention. Their challenge is that they accentuate the researcher–researched relationship in ways already discussed. Many researchers, however, have worked with this challenge, paying closer attention to setting up the room in a playful manner, engaging the child immediately in a nonthreatening and fun activity, and working positively toward a successful encounter.

Individual interviews are recommended for exploring sensitive or private matters and for going into depth about an experience or issue or if the topic has something to do with how each child understands the topic of inquiry or engages with the material. Studies that have used individual interviews have explored helpful and harmful relationships in the lives of 5- to 14-year-olds (Rogers et al., 2005), perceptions of classroom writing with elementary-age students (Cappello, 2005), and views of disability in school with 7- to 10-year-olds (Holt, 2004).

Interview studies often use other methods such as participant observation to get a fuller picture of the context of the inquiry and build rapport with children before inviting them to participate in an interview. Studies that solely use interviews may use multiple interviews to allow time for the relationship between interviewer and interviewee to develop. The study by Rogers et al. (2005) on children's perceptions of their personal and social relationships is one such report. In that study, two to three interviews were conducted annually for 3 years.

> In the first interview, we did not use a prearranged protocol. We went to meet the children with drawing materials, cards, jokes, puppets, and ourselves, hoping first to form a relationship in which children could begin to trust us enough to tell us something real about their lives . . . . Interviewers followed the child's stories and play, rather than setting the agenda. In the second interview, we drew upon developmental materials (art materials and particular questions designed for specific age groups) to create an individually tailored interview based on the first interview. (Rogers et al., 2005, p. 158)

Interviewing is a flexible data-collection method that accomplishes much in a 15-minute block of time or an hour. When designing interview studies, one needs to consider the who, how many, how often, how long, when, where, and why of the study and then remain open to making alterations when necessary. Sometimes a friend or a parent is invited to sit in on the interview because it makes sense to the researcher perhaps as a way to reduce researcher–participant power inequalities (Mayall, 2000) or because, if the interview is occurring in the home, not to give a child the choice to have his or her parent present seems unethical (Barker & Weller, 2003). The consequences of these decisions are varied, but one of them is that the researcher is no longer conducting individual interviews and the data analysis needs to reflect that. For example, when parents and children are interviewed together, there may be disagreement, with parents contradicting or correcting their children or vice versa, thus making interpretation of the child's perspective more difficult.

GROUP INTERVIEWS OR FOCUS GROUPS

Group interviews that focus on a common topic, engage children with a common set of activities, or bring together participants who have had a common experience or life situation are suitable for children of all ages (Darbyshire, MacDougall, & Schiller, 2005; Hennessy & Heary, 2005; Mauthner, 1997; M. Morgan et al., 2002). We do not differentiate between focus groups and group interviews and use the terms interchangeably. We use the term "focus group" broadly, like D. L. Morgan (1997), to mean "a research technique that collects data through group interaction on a topic determined by the researcher" (p. 6). In fact, it is because of the qualities it offers of being a group that makes this approach appealing to researchers working with children. A focus group is less conducive to getting to know individual children's experiences in depth, but it offers other opportunities for understanding their experiences. They are not, however, a substitute for multiple individual interviews, because the group interaction is seen as a crucial component in the generation of data. "Instead of asking questions of each person in turn, focus group researchers encourage participants to talk to one another: asking questions, exchanging anecdotes, and commenting on each others' experiences and points of view" (Kitzinger & Barbour, 1999, p. 4).

In some situations, the group dynamic is the focal point for the research. As children come together in conversation, they engage their social and cultural worlds as they interact together, agree and disagree, laugh, or get upset. Studies that focus on particular group dynamics, such as families or friendship groups, are ones in which group interviews may be useful, because the usual patterns of negotiation, communication, and control are likely to arise during the interview. In other situations, the collective knowledge of the group is of interest and is, in fact, seen as conducive to constructing that collective knowledge. "Group interviews grow directly out of peer culture, as children construct their meanings collectively with their peers. In group interviews . . . participants build on each other's talk and discuss a wider range of experiences and opinions than may develop in individual interviews" (Eder & Fingerson, 2003, p. 35).

Focus groups are often used to get a sense of some aspect of children's collective viewpoint or lived experience. The idea is not so much to hear what different individuals have to say but to engage the group in generating knowledge about a topic with which they have had direct experience. For example, Veale (2005) used focus groups with 7- to 17-year-old displaced Rwandan children. The groups, which were called workshops, "served the more specific function of engaging [children] in an analysis and articulation of their perspectives on the lives of children in the community" (p. 255). The process involved giving children, who had lost much, a space to share their experience, voice their anger and grief, and act out their beliefs through stories and role-playing. The activities they used, including social mapping, story games, drawings, and drama, were meant "to facilitate reflection, debate, argument, dissent and consensus, to stimulate the articulation of multiple voices and positions, and through the process, to lay the foundations for empowerment" (p. 254). If you think of the differences metaphorically, an individual interview might resemble more of a funnel, where the researcher follows up on the interviewee's story asking for more detail of the experience just shared, whereas a group interview is more of a series of sunbursts, with each experience shared eliciting a variety of related ones.

Many researchers believe group interviews engage children because they diminish the effects of adult power, reduce the pressure on individuals to answer questions, and provide support from others in the group (Hennessy & Heary, 2005; Mauthner, 1997). However, power and status differences play out among children as well and affect the interaction and contribution of each member. Hurworth et al. (2005) caution researchers to pay attention and observe the interactions and the way meaning is negotiated because "it is possible that one or two of the more vocal participants may have influenced the discussion and swayed the 'shared' consensus of the group" (p. 59).

The interactive nature of the focus group can work to enhance the input of children, or it can interfere with the ability for all children to find a voice. For example, our final activity in the second group interview we conducted with fourth graders was to have each child finish the sentence "I am glad the ELA is over because . . . ." Corbin, one of the students in our suburban group, restlessly waited for his turn as we went around the circle. However, when it was his turn, he had been listening, and said:

> "*I am glad the ELA is over because* . . . um, like Morgan, Lynn, and Megan, I don't like taking notes from a book or something and, um, like you know, it's kind of like if you're practicing for a play, I don't like to, if I'm in a play I don't like to do skits that, um, like are there for me. I like to, you know, make up my own skits. But, um, it's kind of like dirt biking freestyle, or monster truck freestyle, and also it's because like I don't like, like David said, I don't like the real, I like the real test, because the real test is actually what your grade is really getting graded on. And because we only take three sessions of the real test and like we take like, on each session, we do like, um, at least three pretests, so it's like more than nine pretests. And when we do the real test we only do three sessions."

Our urban fourth graders were also listening to each other, but in this excerpt (which should not be read as indicative of their overall behavior in our sessions together) they are restless and interrupt each other.

AMBER: *I am glad the ELA is over because* . . . shut up! (*directed at other students who are talking over her*)

VINCENT: Because "shut up"? (*teasing*)

JAKE: (*Amber's brother, to Amber, who makes a face at Vincent*): Watch when we go home, I'll take you on my knee.

RESEARCHER: Let her answer.

AMBER: It was hard. There.

JAKE: *I am glad the ELA is over because* . . . it was boring.

VINCENT: That's what I was going to say.

Interpersonal interaction is generally seen as an advantage of focus groups; however, it is important to consider the role of group processes in determining the nature of that interaction and to recognize that such interactions are not always positive. There is the possibility that intimidation within the group may inhibit some individuals from making a contribution (Lewis, 1992). There is also a possibility that an individual's expressed opinion may be influenced by a desire to fit in with other group members (Hennessy & Heary, 2005).

Focus groups present unique challenges, and they are more difficult to schedule because they require a time and place everyone can get to. They also create confidentiality issues because information shared in a group could be repeated outside the group. One strategy is to let participants know that it is not alright to share what was disclosed in any detail outside the group but to talk in general about what was said. Although this is a strategy that can work for some children, understanding the sociocultural dynamics of the group you are working with is important. Holding young participants responsible for confidentiality may cause anxiety because they may not share the researcher's criterion for what should not be shared. Furthermore, what might cause embarrassment among children may be very different from what adults think causes embarrassment. It seems that if the topic of discussion is too sensitive to be repeated, then it may not be appropriate for a group situation, especially among children who may interact regularly. Conducting groups with children who do not regularly interact may be an option. Other strategies include reminding children before beginning the focus group to share only information they would be comfortable sharing with an acquaintance or limiting the group to same-sex friendship groups.

Punch (2002a) reported that her decision to conduct same-sex groups, when exploring 13- and 14-year-olds' perceptions of their problems, welfare, and coping strategies, was based on the literature indicating that girls and boys deal and talk about their problems differently. Just because a focus group is a group event does not preclude creating space for individual responses. We had students answer questions quietly and in writing. Although we had students pass their answers around so that others could write their responses beneath the others as a way of giving students a chance to respond, reflect, or disagree with what others had said, this activity could be adapted by not sharing the writing to create a private space for participants' comments.

In designing any study, every component should be considered for what it adds and also for what it replaces. Depending on the research goals, researchers use multiple approaches within one methodological approach, such as focus groups, or include multiple methods, such as conducting both individual and group interviews with the same participants. In her study of eighth-grade girls in school, Orenstein (1994) conducted focus groups and individual interviews to get a better sense of the breadth and depth of the issues facing young adolescent girls. In addition, Michell (1999) compared the responses of 11-year-old girls given in group and individual interviews and concluded that, depending on the social status of the girl (higher, medium, or low), the responses between the two interview settings were markedly different. Michell's findings reinforce our belief that understanding the social context of the group is essential to understanding the interactions and responses given in a focus group.

DISCUSSION QUESTIONS

1. We often see ourselves as needing to teach or guide young people. Sit with a child and talk to him or her as if he or she was the expert of his or her life or some aspect of life. Ask the child to talk about something important or interesting to him or her. How easy or hard was it for the child to talk to you? How easy or hard was it for you to let him or her take the lead in the conversation? What do you think made it easy or hard? What could you do differently to turn the interaction into a genuine conversation?

2. Develop an interview protocol of about 10 questions you would like to ask your child participants. Consider other approaches beyond open-ended interview questions for each question such as writing tasks, games, photoelicitation strategies, or mapping. Share these with a partner. Rework the protocol based on insights developed in your conversation.

CHAPTER 7

Art and Photography

Images seem to speak to the eye, but they are really addressed
to the mind. They are ways of thinking, in the guise of ways of
seeing. The eye can sometimes be satisfied with form alone,
but the mind can only be satisfied with meaning, which can be
contemplated, more consciously or less, after the eye is closed.
—Duff (1975, p. 12)

Wilson Duff, a media theorist, was referring to Northwest Coast
indigenous sculpture, but understanding the meaning of form and
images and their role in human societies applies to all visual forms:
There is more to understanding them than the eye can see. In Chapter 6, we described the use of visual materials such as photos and
videos to elicit verbal responses in interviews with young people.
We continue that discussion by exploring the use of participant-
produced images such as drawings, photographs, and maps as data.
After a brief overview of the use of images in social science research,
we provide specific examples of the ways drawing, photography, and
mapping can be incorporated into research designs.

VISUAL FORMS OF EXPRESSION AND REPRESENTATION

Images are all around us; we are all image makers and image readers. Images are a rich source of data for understanding the social

world and for representing our knowledge of that social world. Image-based research has a long history in cultural anthropology and sociology as well as the natural sciences but is nonetheless still relatively uncommon (Collier & Collier, 1986). Images should not be romanticized, but neither should their value as data and knowledge be ridiculed or avoided. Especially in Western industrialized cultures, images are often associated with artistic expression, entertainment, and persuasion. Images are seen as intuitive, representing implicit and subjective knowledge, whereas numeric, text, and verbal data are more associated with fact, reason, and objective knowledge. Images, in fact, are no more suspect than any other sort of data, such as numbers or text. Images, like any data, can be used to lie, question, imagine, critique, theorize, mislead, flatter, hurt, unite, narrate, explain, teach, and represent.

Image-based research includes found, researcher-generated, or participant-produced video, photographs, drawings, cartoons, maps, and other visual forms of expression and representation. The use of images has increased over the years as being valid data as well as being part of alternative approaches to representing research results, because they offer a different form through which researchers and participants can express their experience and present themselves to others (Chaplin, 1994; Prosser, 1998; Rose, 2001).

Photography, whether researcher or participant produced, provides a way to document a world viewed and experienced by the photographer. It provides a snapshot of a world or culture of interest that can then be used to support, augment, and illustrate the analysis or perspectives of groups or individuals. The classic example is Margaret Mead and Gregory Bateson's photographic study of Balinese life (Mead & Bateson, 1942). This book includes 759 still photographs with captions, including the context of the photos complemented by theoretical discussion. Mead and Bateson were motivated to move beyond what Mead described as "ordinary English words" because of their inadequacy for capturing and communicating the emotions of the South Sea Islanders; photography and film became their alternate grammar. Today, photography is often no longer sought out for its objective representation of the world but for its power to focus the eye (and the mind) and evoke emotions. It is seen as a legitimate form of expression for researchers as well as participants, as we discuss later in this chapter.

Art, on the other hand, has been on an alternate path. Seen as deeply subjective and as something created from the inside that is of significance to the artist, it has been used in more controlled ways with specific rules about what could or could not be interpreted from its content. For example, too much could be read into the size of a house or the absence of a father, and patterns and themes would have to be established over several drawings. It has only recently been that the use of drawing as an alternative way to communicate everyday experience has gained favor in the social sciences.

COMMUNICATING THROUGH PARTICIPANT DRAWINGS

Long before children attend school, most will have made use of all of their senses, incorporating the various symbol systems presented to them in the different material resources within their world. It makes sense then to use these different symbolic resources when we engage with children and seek to understand their experiences.

The use of drawings when working with, representing, or research-ing children and young people is not new. In child psychology, art has received special attention as a way to document and understand chil-dren's normal artistic development (see, e.g., Kellogg, 1970). Art has also been studied alongside other cognitive processes. For example, in his 1947 *Creative and Mental Growth,* Viktor Lowenfeld describes children's drawing and their connection to specific facets of intellec-tual growth. Art also has a long history in psychiatric consultations as a means to connect to the unconscious of the individual or to tap into the emotional world of the patient (see, e.g., Winnicott, 1971).

In anthropology, researchers have sought to understand the impact of culture on children's artistic production, switching the focus from the artist and his or her art to the artist encultured in par-ticular ways. Alland (1983), along with many anthropologists in the 1970s and 1980s, used cross-cultural comparison in looking for uni-versal cultural patterns. More recently, researchers have looked at the potential of drawings and other human-produced images as a window on culture itself. The study of images as a way into social practices has generated the fast-growing and popular field of visual sociology.

Children's drawings, or other images they may create, neces-sarily represent multiple layers of meanings and values. In an international study asking children to draw fruit trees, the majority of children drew apple trees, even children from countries where such trees do not exist (L. L. Adler, 1982). Adler concluded that children's drawings were influenced by local value systems that were themselves influenced by global images. "Drawing is not a process of imitating or copying the physical world, but rather of synthesizing life experiences. Art then becomes a means through which the child can communicate about those phenomena which are too complex to describe verbally, but which are being perceived and integrated into a child's organization of reality" (McNiff, 1981, p. 29).

Drawing is often portrayed as a natural method for which children have a natural propensity or talent, but children differ in how they respond to this form of expression. Punch (2002b) found that the Bolivian children in her study had limited experience making drawings in school or at home, limited exposure to images, and few material resources to create images. As a result, their drawings contained stylized images of animals and homes. Drawing, like other forms of expression, is learned within particular contexts that shape its use. An advantage children seem to have with drawing is that they are amenable to integrating multiple symbolic forms often in unique and creative ways. For example, children growing up in bilingual or trilingual households not only communicate with speakers of the different languages but comfortably "borrow" a grammatical rule from one language and use it in another. Children are not more capable of drawing than adults, but, as discussed in Chapter 5, they tend to respond enthusiastically to hands-on, interactive experiential activities. Like adults, they too have preferences for which mode of communication they use.

Using drawing in nontherapeutic situations to elicit children's everyday experiences is a fairly recent phenomenon that is gaining popularity across disciplines. In education, Kendrick and McKay (2004) solicited drawings of Canadian elementary students on their experiences of reading and writing in school, Wheelock et al. (2000) asked students of all ages across Massachusetts to draw themselves taking the state standardized tests, and Weber and Mitchell (2000) had children from three different countries draw images of teachers. In leisure studies, Yuen (2004) used drawings to focus interviews with 11-year-old campers at an international camp, while Punch (2002b) had Bolivian children draw pictures of their houses and communities.

Cox's (2005) work on young children's drawings challenges the assumption made by stage theorists that artistic development follows predictable stages and necessarily progresses toward realistic depictions of reality. "When the purpose of drawing is no longer tied to the assumed intention to depict the world, as it is 'neutrally' seen, a new perspective is opened up. We can look at children's drawing, not so much in terms of categorizing the artifacts, which are produced, but in terms of looking at the activities that produce them and at the children who are engaging in those activities. It shifts the focus towards what is going on when children draw" (p. 118). This is not to suggest that children are not depicting real events, objects, or experiences, but that children, just as adults do, use representation to express an emotion, idea, or experience in creative, playful, or abstract ways. Drawing offers a different symbolic mode to explore and use and, like dialogue, fits nicely within a social constructivist view of the world. "The role which children's drawing plays is a constructive one. Through it, children purposefully bring shape and order to their experience, and in so doing, their drawing activity is actively defining reality, rather than passively reflecting a 'given' reality" (Cox, 2005, p. 124).

Drawing as a mode of sense making and representation offers different possibilities than talk alone does. Drawing can cut through "the levels of pretence, posing, and edited self-presentation" (Schratz & Walker, 1995, p. 80) that often accompany verbal responses. Interviews or other language-based data-collection methods demand a response in a time-sensitive way, but creative tasks like drawing may be approached more leisurely, thus giving children time to think more reflectively about what to produce as a response (Gauntlett, 2005). Figure 7.1 provides an overview of the different reasons for using drawing in research and the value of using drawings.

Individual Drawing

In general, studies that include the elicitation of drawing from individual children or young people give specific directions, most often in the form of a prompt or question. For example, Yuen (2004) asked 11-year-old children attending an international camp to draw the answers to four questions: "(1) How would you describe our camp community?; (2) How did you communicate with others?; (3) Think of the activities we did at camp and what you learned from them; and

Ways to Use Drawing in Research
- As an icebreaker or warm-up to build rapport.
- To give participants and researchers a common focus.
- To help quieter or shyer participants feel more comfortable and engaged with the research situation.
- To focus or refocus a conversation.
- To tap into visual and emotional meanings.
- To provide time to reflect on the topic or question.
- To provide an alternative form of representation.
- To reduce the influence of a group on its members.
- For data triangulation.

Reasons for Using Drawing in Research
- Drawings reveal participant feelings and emotions.
- Drawing leads to a succinct presentation of the key elements of participants' experiences.
- Drawings are especially valuable when combined with additional interpretation provided by participants.
- Limited structure in the drawing activity allows participants' unique experiences, rather than researcher constructs, to be communicated.

FIGURE 7.1. Ways to use drawings and reasons to do so.

(4) Think about what you did during Free Time, what you learned and why it was important to you?" In our study of fourth- and eighth-grade students' experiences with state-mandated testing, we asked fourth graders to remember how they felt taking the ELA test and to draw themselves feeling that feeling. We had the students share their drawings with us and the group. Figures 7.2, 7.3, 7.4, and 7.5 are examples of those drawings and include the verbal description provided by the students.

Using drawings in individual or group interviews is not the only or most typical ways drawings are collected in a study. Many researchers take advantage of institutional settings such as schools to have teachers give the prompt and collect the drawings. This approach has the advantage of being able to collect a larger sample of drawings but has the disadvantage of not allowing the researcher to hear from each participant about his or her drawing. Youth can, of course, write their interpretations of their drawings for a distant researcher (Weber & Mitchell, 2000; Wheelock et al., 2000).

FIGURE 7.2. Lena: "[I was feeling] scared."

FIGURE 7.3. Lynn: "I drew a picture of myself talking to myself. I said don't get scared and I can do this. And then I said I'm almost done and I'm going to do well."

FIGURE 7.4. Jake: "I was shaking. I was nervous. I'm like I'm not ready for it. I hope I pass."

FIGURE 7.5. Corbin: "I drew me doing my test. And at the time I thought I was gonna do good because like on all the other pretests I got good grades and like on every one I got a B+ and higher. And I came to school and ate well and slept well and all that. And I really felt confident in myself."

Group Drawing

Just as group interviews are a mixture of individual and collective contributions to the meaning-making process, having young people draw in groups provides a way for them to depict shared experiences with a particular topic. In addition, just as in group interviews, different groups will exhibit different styles of collaboration, issues, and outcomes, and individuals in groups will display different levels and styles of involvement in their groups. Unlike verbal exchanges, however, group drawing asks for an explicit outcome, in this case a pictorial representation of their shared experience that they must negotiate and consider together. Group drawing, therefore, moves beyond telling us something about the group through a group-created product and also gives a glimpse at how each group works together to negotiate the meaning-making process itself.

Figure 7.6 provides an example of a group drawing. We asked fourth graders to think of their teacher doing a test preparation activity and then draw that activity. We explained that they could each draw whatever they wanted or they could create a story by drawing together. From left to right, Tracy, a European American female, Savannah, an African American female, and Faith, a Hispanic American female, worked together. They quickly decided that they would

FIGURE 7.6. Fourth graders Tracy, Savannah, and Faith.

119

draw and worry about the story later. This is an excerpt of their con-versation while drawing:

> SAVANNAH: Can I draw my teacher handing me—with like a big smile on my face when he's giving me—the paper?
>
> RESEARCHER: Yeah, but maybe you should talk to see if you want to do a story line or if you want to do three different pic-tures.
>
> FAITH: I was just going to say, "How about we talk it over?"
>
> [Researcher walks away from this team, leaving the tape recorder on the floor next to them, which they notice and use to narrate their process. Although they were not instructed to talk while they draw and only to talk to figure out what they will draw, these students may have heard it as both.]
>
> TRACY: So why don't you draw on this side. Why don't you draw your teacher giving you a paper, you draw your teacher giv-ing you a paper.
>
> SAVANNAH: First, we got to draw the story.
>
> FAITH: First, we got to draw a picture. This is the first one.
>
> TRACY: The picture needs to match the story.
>
> SAVANNAH: No.
>
> TRACY: Not really.
>
> FAITH: Well, look, I'm going to start.
>
> TRACY: Well, we are going to write. What are we going to write about?
>
> SAVANNAH: No, she said we could just draw or write or just make bubbles. What do you want to do?
>
> FAITH: Draw.
>
> TRACY: Let's draw first.
>
> FAITH: And make bubbles.
>
> TRACY: Yeah! We're going to draw and make bubbles. We are going to draw a picture and make bubbles. Faith, take over. (*Hands Faith the tape recorder.*)
>
> FAITH: For my picture I am drawing my math teacher Mr. . . . giv-ing me my ELA test, Savannah.

SAVANNAH: For my picture I am drawing me and my teacher giving me a great look because I am doing well on my ELA practice test.

TRACY: Hello, my name is Tracy, and I am going to draw me, and my friends are going to draw bubble words and draw of how our teacher's giving us a paper and doing something.

(*They repeat some of this information and tell us their ages.*)

TRACY: We are going to work very hard on this effort because we are friends and we are going to be doing a very big large team work.

FAITH: Teamwork. From Faith, Tracy, and Savannah. OK, one, two, three (*They all call out together*): Teamwork!

(*They continue to work as they discuss the details of their drawing together and then at the end they read what they wrote in the tape recorder.*)

Group activities such as this prompt a different kind of interaction. It is clear that these fourth graders need to negotiate a number of things: the personalities within the group (especially if they might not have known each other before the focus group), the task at hand and how they will go about fulfilling it, the expectations of a research project, and interpreting the directions given about the different tasks. The girls not only feel comfortable enough with the situation to play with the recorder, but they use it in appropriate ways to narrate what they perceive as their team's work. Later, however, they get carried away describing details of their drawings to each other and laugh embarrassedly as they make a comment that they do not feel is appropriate for the recorder. Perhaps to make up for this faux pas, they take up the recorder again and read what they have written in their bubbles, concluding with them saying in chorus, "This is all about the ELA. Thank you for listening to Tracy, Savannah, and Faith. Bye. We're done."

The quality of the recording equipment is key to the success of this type of data collection, and the care in taping is directly related to the nature of the planned data analysis. Even though we kept track of who worked with whom in small groups, recognizing who was speaking during transcription of the tapes proved difficult. If identification of individual speakers is important, video recordings or an observer are good strategies for keeping track of who is speak-

> - Provide plain unlined white paper.
> - Have the same drawing tools available for all participants.
> - Avoid awkward paper sizes that are difficult to work with or to reproduce.
> - Test recording equipment if it will be used in conjunction with drawing activities.

FIGURE 7.7. Practical tips when using drawing.

ing. Recording is also more difficult if children are moving about, such as leaning over to get markers, because even small movements create interferences with taping quality. In the prior example, the three girls helped enormously by leaning into the tape recorder and announcing their names, but in other situations we captured only bits and pieces of conversations, especially when two or three small groups in the same room chose to talk across the room to each other. Figure 7.7 provides practical tips if drawings will be collected as data.

COMMUNICATING THROUGH PHOTOGRAPHS AND VIDEO

The emphasis on the elicitation of participants' own meanings and experiences has prompted researchers to hand participants cameras to take pictures or video relevant to the research topic. Called auto-driving (Heisley & Levy, 1991), reflexive photography (Douglas, 1998), photo novella (Wang & Burris, 1994), and PhotoVoice (Wang & Burris, 1997), the focus is on using the images to elicit commentary in written form or in face-to-face interviews. Auto-driven photography approaches give children ownership of the dialogue through selection of their own photographs. Allowing children to participate in taking, selecting, and then talking about photographs is often meant to promote critical dialogue, empowerment, and decision making among research participants (Hurworth, 2003).

The most common strategy for using photography with children is to equip them with cameras to take pictures in their communities, schools, or homes related to the study topic. Their pictures become the basis for individual or group interviews. Such studies have had children take pictures of spaces of physical activity for health research (Darbyshire et al., 2005), their daily lives (Punch, 2002b), neighborhood spaces (Smith & Barker, 2002), and important things in the nursery (Clark, 2004). In her work with 3- and 4-year-olds, Clark (2004) shows that young children are capable of using a camera and take pride in talking about the pictures they took.

PhotoVoice is a popular participatory approach that provides children a tool to speak out about their lives and is used in a variety of international empowerment and development projects. "PhotoVoice offers marginalized groups, including many children, the skills of 'participatory photography,' visual literacy, and a powerful universal language to express their ideas and represent their realities to the rest of us" (Gavin, 2003). (See *www.photovoice.org/html/projects/photovoiceprojects* to view a number of these PhotoVoice projects.) Imaging the world is placed in the hands of those who typically have the least access to creating images (in contrast to media images, e.g., which are created by corporations), and those grassroots images become compelling direct evidence for targeting policymakers or others in a position to promote change. Photographs are chosen to communicate collective assets and concerns, which are then contextualized with stories about those photographs. The dialoguing or storytelling about the images provides the basis for lobbying for or recommending ameliorative action. Additionally, images created through PhotoVoice are sometimes sold to generate income for the photographers themselves. The emphasis on enabling children to define for themselves what is worth knowing, remembering, and changing makes PhotoVoice consistent with a social constructivist perspective coupled with an action research orientation.

With youth's increased technological sophistication, digital communications have become a natural way for children to communicate and capture their experiences. Indeed, social networking websites (such as Facebook and MySpace), video sites (such as YouTube), and text and instant messaging have become routine means for communication among youth. Mathison is currently conducting a study with young teens using video taken by them with cell phones to capture leisure activities. Their videos show them at school dances, engaged in social interaction with one another, skateboarding, playing basketball, even engaged in illicit activity like drawing graffiti. These young teenagers routinely take both photographs and videos with their cell phones, information that they share with one another and that provides useful data about what the youth do with their time and what they value.

Using child-produced photographs or videos gives children and youth flexibility and freedom to choose what is important and what to depict. It makes sense, however, to provide some direction, but the specificity depends on the research questions. The focus can be quite broad, such as asking children to take pictures of their daily lives or, as in the example of the cell phone videos described previously, simply asking teens to share whatever videos they wish. Punch (2002b) found that children took pictures of exciting events (such as street fights) or seasonal events (such as potato crops) because those were occurring at that time. On the other hand, the researcher may provide more specific instructions, such as asking children to take pictures of the spaces where they participated in physical activities (Darbyshire et al., 2005), which helps children focus on something specific (e.g., yards, parks, playgrounds).

COMMUNICATING THROUGH MAPS

Mapping, or graphically representing one's social or physical environment, has been used in development research, geography, social psychology, and health as a way to elicit a young person's perception of some aspect of their environment (Morrow, 2001, 2003). (See Figure 7.8 for an illustration of a map drawn by a child.) Children as young as 4 years have the spatial capacity for mapping activities (Blaut, Stea, Spencer, & Blades, 2003; Darbyshire et al., 2005). As with drawing, mapping has been used as an elicitation device for individual or group interviews. For example, Darbyshire et al. (2005) asked 4- to 12-year-old children in the context of focus groups on children's perceptions of physical activity to map out the places where they usually participated in physical activity. Child-made maps "can provide valuable insight for others into children's everyday environment because it is based on the features they consider important, and hence can lead to good discussion about aspects of their lives that might not so easily emerge in words" (Hart, 1997, quoted in Clark, 2004, p. 146).

During the 2002 United Nations International Children's Conference on the Environment, Blanchet-Cohen, Ragan, and Amsden (2003) used mapping as a way to bring 400 10- to 12-year-olds, repre-

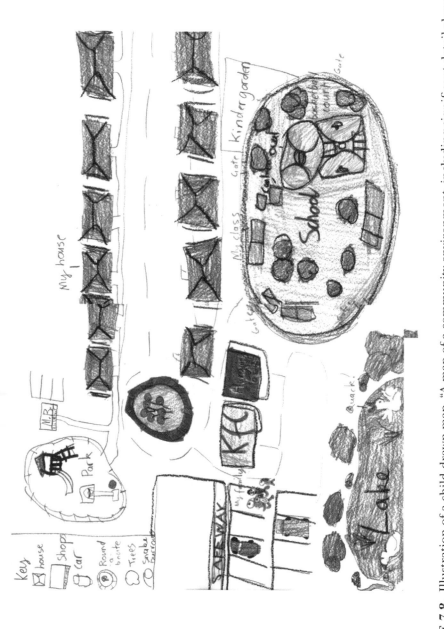

FIGURE 7.8. Illustration of a child-drawn map. "A map of a community environment, including significant detail about destinations in the local neighborhood and demonstrating opportunities for physical activities as well as social interaction." From Hume, Salmon, and Ball (2005). Copyright 2005 by Oxford University Press. Reprinted by permission.

senting 60 countries, together to collectively voice their concerns and ideas about environmental issues. The mapping activities included thematic maps, such as healthy communities and climate change, and body maps, where one child's body was traced and the outline filled with drawings and statements of concern to the children. "A key aspect of maps is that they are relational—they represent the relationships between spatial/physical elements, cultural values and abstract ideas. . . . In child-created maps, a child offers a glimpse into his or her worldview, where the boundaries between the emotional, social and cognitive perspectives merge" (Blanchet-Cohen et al., 2003).

PLANNING FOR VISUAL ACTIVITIES

When to introduce drawings, photography, or mapping in individual or group interviews is dependent on what you hope your study and the young people will gain from this activity. No less than any other data-collection strategy, it is important that the data collection is appropriate for the research questions and is compelling to the participants. Visual activities often take more time and resources (drawing supplies, cameras) than other forms of data collection.

In our work with fourth graders, we closed the first interview with the group drawing activity mentioned previously. We did this as a wrap-up activity to allow the children to think about and put down on paper some of the themes we had talked about. In the second group interview, we began the meeting having students remember how they felt the previous week taking the ELA and draw that feeling. We did this before talking with the children because we wanted to tap into their individual emotions when thinking about the test and did not want our discussion or other children's perceptions to influence that. We then used their drawings to elicit other kinds of information such as the test-taking strategies they used. Just as with any tool, drawing can help guide where the dialogue will go, but it can interfere as well.

Drawing is time consuming, and when children like to draw, they also usually like to take their time with it. In her focus groups with 11-year-old campers, Yuen (2004) asked each participant to draw four pictures. Then, during the focus groups, she had each child present his or her first picture to the group, and when everyone had presented the first picture (including the adults, who also drew their own pictures) they would discuss that topic and then go on to the next picture. Yuen allocated about 30 minutes for the children to draw and then 45 minutes for the discussion period. She explained that, although this was very time consuming, it proved to be a valuable method for soliciting and understanding the children's experiences at camp.

PLANNING FOR ANALYSIS OF VISUAL DATA

As with any type of data, it is important to consider how the images are to be analyzed. In some studies, the intent may be to compare drawings across respondents, such as asking students to draw how they felt taking the test the week before. However, in other studies, the breadth of possibilities for what the participant might draw or how they go about their drawing may mean that cross-participant analysis is more difficult. Wheelock et al. (2000), for example, were limited in what they could conclude from analyzing the self-portraits they had collected from student test takers across Massachusetts because they were not able to meet individual students and the variables affecting each student's experience of taking the test were too plentiful.

As the prior examples show, images can convey meaning in powerful, accessible, and direct ways. The *Kids with Cameras* projects are an example of photographs as direct representation, made popular by the movie *Born into Brothels*. Although this project promotes photography as an empowering skill that will benefit these children, their photographs stand as a representation of their life, a representation that needs no further interpretation or embellishment. The idea is that participant photography is a research strategy that permits participants to speak directly and thus be empowered to influence their community as well as decision makers and policymakers. However, researchers are more likely to see images as no more direct representations of experience than a sentence is without further interpretation. Participants can use drawing and photography to capture meanings beyond words and without words, but words certainly help to situate the expressive meaning of the drawing within a specific framework and context. "Knowledges are conveyed through all sorts of different media, including senses other than the visual, and . . . visual images very often work in conjunction with other kinds of representations. It is very unusual, for example, to encounter a visual image unaccompanied by any text at all, whether spoken or written" (Rose, 2001, p. 10).

Most researchers have used images in conjunction with other information, especially participants' verbal commentary on their images. In a discussion that we take up again in Chapter 9, one reason for this is the general mistrust in the social sciences in researchers' competence in interpreting images that they have not themselves taken or created. In addition, the strategies for judging the trustworthiness of images are not so widely understood. However, images are no more suspect than words and their credibility can be established with attention to (1) the overall quality of the research design, (2) the context, (3) the adequacy of the image from multiple perspectives, and (4) the contribution images make to new knowledge (Mathison, 2008).

DISCUSSION QUESTIONS

1. Buy a disposable camera or use a digital one. Pick a topic of interest to you and take pictures that best represent the kinds of questions you are hoping to explore. Reflect on the experience. How did having to think visually add to or alter your perception or understanding of the topic? What kinds of decisions did you find yourself making about representing your understanding through images? Now give a disposable camera to a young person and ask them to take pictures around the same topic or theme. Process the pictures and then meet with your volunteer and ask her or him to describe his or her process for thinking of and taking the pictures. How similar or different was this process from your own? What might have contributed to these differences or similarities?

2. Purchase a popular magazine geared toward young people. Take note of the content of the articles and pictures, the way they are displayed on the page, and the overall effect of the presentation of image and text. What does an analysis of the content tell you about prevailing assumptions and beliefs about the intended audience?

3. Think of five ways drawing might be incorporated in your research
   design and the reason for its incorporation. Do not limit yourself to
   drawing as data; how might it enhance the development of relationships between participants or between participant and researchers?
   How might it contribute to triangulation of meaning in relation to
   other forms of data collection? Share your outline with a partner.
   Rework based on insights developed in your conversation.

CHAPTER 8

Journaling and Other Written Responses

Helen, one of the urban eighth graders in our study of high-stakes testing, used her journal in a way that researchers dream about when they choose journaling as a data-collection method. She filled every page of three 80-page 5″ × 8″ notebooks with drawings, cartoons, and narrative accounts of her perceptions of and experiences with school, teachers, testing, sports, and being Chinese (see Figures 8.1 and 8.2). She starts off by introducing herself as a 13-year-old with a mother, father, and older brother. She writes that she likes to swim and draw and that science is her favorite subject. She mentions how concerned she was on hearing her name during morning announcements, only to find out she was being congratulated for winning the 100-yard backstroke and 50-yard butterfly swim relay. Here are a few of her entries about the ELA test.

Jan 11th

    The first day of the ELA's is Tuesday. I'm going to sleep at 9:00 that night so I'm well rested for tomorrow. Since tomorrow's test seems to be based on "skills" there is realy no point of studying since I have no clue what's on it. English is not my favorite subject but it's very important. I usually speak Chinese at home so I sometimes mix up the two. For math I know my multiplication in Chinese. Well that's how I rember it. Its hard for me to speak English well. I still have troble spelling, reading and sometimes speaking it. I started learning English on the first day of kindergarten. That means for ½ of the years in P. School [kindergarten–fifth grade] I didn't know anything my teacher was talking about—but one thing I did well was to play the violin. This is the 5th year that I played the violin as an instrument in school. Its something that you don't need to learn how to speak. You just move your bow and make music.

*   *   *

Jan 12th 04

I still have to finish my science homework and Spanish. Tommorrow is part one of the ELA's. I hope nothing goes wrong. I really don't like takeing tests especially when teachers express how important it is. It makes me worrie even more and that's not a very good thing.

I think teachers should not express it as the most importantest thing in the world. It makes me nervos and I think if you fail it ou won't die or something.

?   ?   ?   ?   ?   ?   ?   ?   ?   ?   ?

*   *   *

Such entries, intermingled with sketches and cartoons, gave us insight into many aspects of Helen's life, both in school and out. Although other eighth graders were not as prolific as Helen, each journal had a unique quality to it. Luke, a white, urban student wrote minimally (see Figures 8.3 and 8.4), and yet he addressed similar themes:

Test Day 1

The test was easy. But if I could change 2 things I'd change the # of Breaks + the amount of TIME WE got.

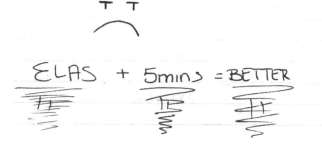

Jan 14th 04

I think they should add 5 mins to each part of the test. The reason is I didn't have time to check it. I finished on the last second for each essay. I didn't get to go back and check my test.
If I did I know I would have found mistakes.

ELAS + 5mins = BETTER

FIGURE 8.1. Helen's journal entry—"5 More Minutes."

FIGURE 8.2. Helen—"Worries I Have."

133

FIGURE 8.3. Luke's Journal Entry—"No Time."

FIGURE 8.4. Luke—"After the ELA."

Test Day 2

Today the test was a sinch. The 2nd long essay (the personal one) was awesome.

It was the Best out of all of them. The only bad thing was NO BREAK.

Week 1

AFTER TEST

English class is a lot more fun. We are doing fun stuff instead of getting Ready for the exams. We are going to Read the Pearl. It will be cool.

Day 2 Week 1

This chapter looks at the strengths of and challenges of collecting written data from children and adolescents. After briefly exploring the theoretical thinking on writing versus speaking as a form of expression, we discuss how writing can be used as a data-collection strategy in research with children.

COMMUNICATING THROUGH WRITING

Writing and speaking are both modes of communication and meaning making and, although related, can function in similar or different ways depending on the social practice, conventions, and purposes within which they are used. At times, writing is seen simply as a system of visual marks representing speech, whereas at other times speech and writing are understood as two distinct cognitive processes. "Speaking and writing differ considerably—in syntactic and linguistic formulations, in rhetorical patterning, in situational context—and in cultural, developmental, and physiological ways" (Halpern, 1982, p. 464). A common view of how writing differs from speaking is that "the primary considerations in conveying meaning in writing are probably (1) developing one's thinking in detail and in a coherent manner and (2) organizing one's statements so as to anticipate the readers' need to know where one is coming from and going to" (Farrell, 1978, p. 347). However, others believe that what Farrell describes is not inherent to writing as a form of communication, but is itself a convention, a use of writing, that is socialized in institutions such as school. Elbow (1985) argues against the prevalent view "that speech and writing are distinctly characterizable media, each of which has its own inherent features and each of which tends to foster a particular cognitive process, or "mentality" (p. 283). Instead, he argues "that each medium can draw on and foster *various* mentalities" (p. 283, emphasis in original).

Elbow turns on its head the usual beliefs about writing. Writing does, as Farrell suggests, promote reflection, organization, and thought, but these qualities are not restricted to writing. Elbow suggests that expectations for and about writing can be expanded and altered by introducing some of the qualities of speech. Similarly, speech can be altered by attending to some of the conventions of writing. For research purposes, writing should not be defined in narrow terms. Writing can take a conventional paragraph or essay form, such as responding to a prompt, or it can take an expressive form, such as in the students' journal entries, where sketches, cartoons, free associative writing, poetry, and responses to questions sit side by side. It is not the mode, writing or speaking, or drawing or photography for that matter, that determines how it is used, but the purpose for its use, the expectations inherent to the conventions of the medium, and the directions given that precipitate its use. "[Writing and speaking are] learned in different ways and at different stages of life, used in different media and different contexts to communicate different information for different purposes to different audiences. . . . But the fact that a form *appears* in one or the other mode does not entail that it belongs to that mode" (Nunberg, 1990, p. 3, emphasis in original). How a writing data-collection activity is structured will play a role in the kind of writing in which the participants engage.

WRITTEN ACCOUNTS AS DATA

Writing can be an individual or a group activity, part of another activity (such as during an interview), or a separate activity in itself, such as keeping a personal journal, as a brief account to describe an event or a more lengthy account narrating a journey or experience. Like other forms of data collection, it offers flexibility of design and can be used for a variety of purposes. Unlike other forms of data collection, however, little has been written about the strengths and challenges of using this approach, except to point out that, like drawing and photography, it puts the pen in the hands of children and thus has the potential to foster a sense of ownership and control over the data.

Writing is a data-collection strategy that can be integrated into children's school routines and is, therefore, relatively easy to use. In her study of how Swedish children conceptualize relationships to place, Halldén (2003) sought the cooperation of teachers in schools in three different towns to elicit narrative accounts of 173 children over a 2-month period on the topic of "My Future Family." As part of an ordinary school assignment, 8- to 14-year-olds were asked by their teachers to "think about a possible future life, to draw a picture of a make-believe family and of the house they could imagine themselves living in when grown up . . . [and then] to write a story about their fictitious families" (p. 34). Over a 2-month period, the children were asked to write on this topic, and each created a personal book of narratives. Halldén used these narratives as the basis for analyzing children's relationships to family, home, and house and their processes for "creating a place of importance" (p. 43).

Writing is also a data-collection activity that children and adolescents can do on their own before, between, or subsequent to other activities, such as group or individual interviews. We asked youth research participants to keep a journal of their experiences with learning and testing as a student in middle school. We did not ask the fourth-grade students to do so, not because we felt they were incapable of keeping a journal but because we felt it was more likely that it would be seen as homework by the parents and interfere unnecessarily in the children's home life. For example, in her study with children in rural Bolivia, Punch (2002b) asked children to write a chronological account of the activities they engaged in the day before. This was a school-based task, but when the children asked if they could continue to write in them at home, she acquiesced. This created conflict in the homes, and parents complained that the children were using the journals as excuses not to do their chores.

As Helen's example shows, journaling can be very successful. Although we had mixed responses, with some students only answering our prompts and others going beyond the prompts, as Helen did, overall the journals gave us unique insight into how each student navigated their lives as students. We gave blank journals to the students in person during their participant assent signing meeting and before our first focus group. Figure 8.5 illustrates the directions we printed inside the front cover of the notebook, along with our first journal prompts.

Writing can also be used as the means for gathering information, which is then used as the focal point for an interview. In her study of how children shape their social lives in urban environments, Zeiher (2003) recruited 10-year-olds in two districts in West Berlin to keep a running log of their daily activities. Children in each district were given notebooks in which they chronicled all their activities from morning until night. After each day, the children were individually

---

General Directions for Using Your Student Journal

1. Your journal is for you to record your experiences with learning and testing as a student in middle school.
2. You are free to write however and whatever you want, although we expect you to write something in it every week. You may draw, write cartoons, write poetry or songs. You may also tell us jokes, anecdotes, "things that happened today"—type of things. Please date your entry.
3. You may be as candid as you would like and use whatever language you would like. These journals will not be shared with your parents or teachers, nor will you be judged in any way on the content of your writing, grammar, spelling, or vocabulary.
4. You may talk about other people, but it is best if you do not use anyone's name; use a description instead: for example, "My social studies teacher . . ." or "A close friend told me. . . ."
5. We will be collecting these journals every 2 or 3 weeks and providing you with a new one.
6. THANK YOU!

First Journal Prompts

1. Who are you? Please describe yourself to us. You may write, draw, write a cartoon, sketch, whatever helps you tell us who you are.
2. What kind of a student do you think you are? How do you think your mother or father see you? What about your teachers?
3. Please keep a log of your test preparation activities.

FIGURE 8.5. Illustration of instructions for journaling.

interviewed. This sequence was repeated seven times over a 2-week period. The children were paid for their participation and seemed proud to be asked for their contribution to the study.

Similarly, writing can be used during an individual or group interview to help focus the conversation. In their study on living with asthma, M. Morgan et al. (2002) asked children in their focus groups to write or draw on large pieces of paper on the floor good and bad things about having asthma. The children's responses were used as the basis for further discussion. Punch (2002a) used a similar activity that she called "Spider Legs." In this activity, she wrote "coping with problems" in the middle of a large sheet of paper and had young people write different ways they could cope, creating a "leg" for each strategy. "Thus, these diagrams were used as a visual aid on which to build information and probe more in-depth" (Punch, 2002a, p. 53).

In focus groups, we have used writing in a variety of ways. In one activity, we gave children several lined sheets of paper with a question or illustration pasted in such a way that, even when the page was turned to the next sheet, you could still see the question. We told the students this was kind of like a chain story in that each student would get a few minutes to read and write out a response before moving the paper and question to the student on their right and receiving the paper and question from the student on their left. There were several reasons why we approached the task this way. The first was that we had several very quiet individuals in both fourth- and eighth-grade urban groups. Most of these students did not speak English as their first language, and finding ways they could comfortably express themselves in a group was necessary. Second, we were not sure how receptive the children would be to writing. In an essay discussing the differences and similarities between speech and writing, Elbow (1985) contrasts children's experiences with learning to speak and learning to write. He concludes that, for the most part, when children start using speech there is immediate recognition and reinforcement that it is speech, whereas when they learn how to write it is often a mixed experience with spelling mistakes pointed out, incorrect word usage and grammar, or poor penmanship. And isn't it often the case, he says, that if you speak out of turn in class, you will be required as a punishment to write "I will not speak in class" 100 times. For this reason, we decided to have the papers rotate among the children. That way the students would not be asked to write for a lengthy period of time, and they were able to see what their classmates wrote, making it interactive and more interesting. This is an example of questions and suburban fourth graders' responses.

Questions:

Was there anything on the ELA that you did not know how to do?

What didn't you know how to do?

Why didn't you know how to do it?

Responses:

"There was nothing on the test that I didn't know. I knew all of the questions. I knew what to do read. I was ready for the test."—LYNN

"I didn't know alot of words. I ast the teacher." —ANDREW

"Their was one word that I didn't recognize. The word was benafit. I figured that it had something to do with teaching other people."— AMANDA

"I don't think that there was anything that I didn't get. I new all the word, and what they ment I think."— DAVID

We also used writing in ways that promoted social interaction. For example, in our third focus group with fourth and eighth graders, conducted in May of their school year, we used a timeline to collect data about what was memorable for fourth and eighth graders looking back at their school year. We wanted to see how much testing stood out in the students' perceptions of the year. As an introduction to the activity, we told students to think back over their year and remember all the things that they did and then to use the long sheet of paper to record the high points and low points of their year. We gave each student a different color marker so we could keep track of who wrote what. We broke the fourth-grade groups into two smaller groups for this activity. The following was what one of the urban fourth-grade groups recorded on their timeline:

September:

"I had the best teacher ever Mr. T."—DAPHNE

"Mrs. T is nice to us sometimes in the class."—AMBER

"We went to the State museum [picture of a carousel]."—ALEXA

October:

"We had a Halloween party [sketch of two girls one saying "happy Halloween"]."—ALEXA

"People used to be bad in our class."—ALEXA

"We did the animal project."—VINCENT

November:

"Is my brothers birthday."—DAPHNE

"On school lunch people would talk and scream loud [sketch of kids sitting at table]."—ALEXA

December/January:

"Went to a play called the Freedom Bound [sketch of figure holding drum]."—DAPHNE

"We measured the volume in are measuring cup [sketch of measuring cup with lines representing nuMBERs up to 150]."—DAPHNE

February/March/April/May:

"My teacher moved to a new job." —VINCENT

"My math teacher Mr. T went to a new job and he is not our math teacher anymore. I wish he could come back. I miss Mr. T [sad face]."—DAPHNE

"In science we learned about floating and sinking."—ALEXA

"My teacher helps me [two girl figures, one saying "thank you"]."—ALEXA

"We measured things [sketch of a balance scale]."—ALEXA

"We had a really bad day in music with a sub [sketch of people and one hitting a drum]."—DAPHNE

"We did floating and sinking and it was fun."—DAPHNE

June:

"We are going to the zoo."—VINCENT

We used a writing task as an icebreaker for our eighth-grade groups that we called "walk-abouts." We created three large sheets of paper and in the center of each was one theme: The School, Teachers and Instruction, and Life as an Eighth Grader. Around the central theme were four questions. Students were given a different color marker and were told to walk around the three tables and answer at least two questions on each sheet. They could also add notes or draw pictures. This is an example of how four suburban students answered the sheet about "Life as an Eighth Grader":

> *Question: The top three things I worry about most when I come to school are . . .*

"If I have done all my homework and if my grades are all good."
    —LEAH

"My friends, my teachers, my classes."—HANNAH

"My teachers, my attitude, my work."—JADE

"Did I bring everything I need."—JOYCE

> *Question: My classmates generally feel . . . about learning.*

"Negatively."—LEAH

> *. . . They show this by . . .*

"Saying it's stupid, and retarded and not doing their work."
    —LEAH

> *Question: The pressure I feel to do my work comes mostly from . . .*

"Teachers and parents."—JADE

"Teachers and parents."—LEAH

> *He/she or it motivates me by . . .*

"Giving me more work and say I'm making myself smarter by doing my work."—JADE

"To do my work the best I can."—LEAH

> *Question: Doing well in eighth grade matters because . . .*

"If you don't do well in 8th grade you don't [do] well in High School and if you don't [do] well in College and if you don't do well in College you don't get a good job."—HANNAH

"You need to get good grades so you get good classes in high
school, go to good colleges and get a good job."—JOYCE

"My parents are more proud of me and I can get into a better
[college]."—JADE

"I won't understand anything in high school and then high
school is the base for college."—LEAH

Writing also offers possibilities for anonymous feedback or questions from participants. Punch (2002a) used a box technique at the
beginning of her group interview with young adolescents on their
views of their problems and coping strategies. She asked the youth to
write down a recent problem and put it in a box. The responses were
varied: two were swearing, one was blank, a few stated that they had
no problems, and many were about sexual issues, puberty, grief, and
illegal activities. Each response gave her some insight into the lives
and issues facing her young participants.

ARTIFACTS

In addition to writing that is explicitly part of the research process,
children and youth write in many contexts, and that writing is an
artifact that is itself data or something that can be used as an elicitation device. It may be that writing contrived for a research study
lacks the authenticity of ways children use writing to communicate,
make meaning, think, and so on (Edelsky, Searfoss, & Mersereau,
1986). When the focus of a research study seeks to understand children's authentic activities, then seeking authentic data is key. For
example, if one wishes to understand the unique vocabulary youth
create for digital communication (e.g., ROFL for "roll on floor laugh-
ing"), then the most appropriate data are actual digital communications (e-mail, instant messages [IM], social networking sites). There
is a vast literature that focuses on student writing per se, which is
not our emphasis; rather, one can understand children and youth
experience through their writing. For example, teenage youth may
combine art and writing in graffiti, a form of writing that is personal but also reflects social relationships and experiences (Abel &
Buckley, 1977). Graffiti tags (stylized signatures) or pieces (artistic
renderings) may be analyzed from a cultural, gendered, linguistic,

folkloric, or aesthetic perspective, any of which take advantage of an artifact to understand how youth make sense of their experiences within modernity.

TECHNOLOGY AND WRITING

Finally, technology offers new possibilities for generating written data that are worth exploring. "New forms of computing technology offer considerable scope for use in research. Children are often more familiar than adults with these media and can use them readily to communicate with others about their lives" (Greene & Hill, 2005, p. 14). Children use various digital media to communicate with one another, a strategy labeled "media multitasking" or the phenomenon of youth simultaneously e-mailing, IMing, playing a video game, listening to music, reading a news story, and so on. A communication strategy like IMing is widely used among youth and presents several opportunities for researchers interested in children's lived experience. The messages themselves and ways in which IMing is used are data. IM can also be a data-collection strategy (e.g., IM as interview). The messages and the practice of IMing are also potential elicitation devices, in the same way any other participant-generated data is used to elicit meaning.

Computer-mediated communications combine aspects of writing and speaking, becoming in essence a conversation in print (Markham, 1998). Practically speaking, e-mail and IM as interview present a number of challenges for researchers, including finding a common platform, planning for synchronous communication across time zones, developing common conventions for communication, and developing clear strategies for downloading and saving data (Mason, 2000). With any data-collection strategy, where something is gained there may be something lost. Computer-mediated communications offer convenience, ease of transcription, accessibility, and participant control over the text of an interview, but at the same time the communicativeness of body language is lost, unique problems of data collection and storage are presented, and potential technological problems may interfere with data collection (Mason, 2002). The ubiquity of computer-mediated communication among children and youth signal that social constructivist researchers need to explore these forms of communication, which are a rich part of the lived experience of those with whom we are interested in doing research.

DISCUSSION QUESTIONS

1. Brainstorm ways you might use writing in a study with young people. Come up with three writing activities to include in the research design and a rationale for their inclusion.

2. Join an online chat group geared toward young people. Pay attention to the way group members use writing as a way to express their thoughts and agree and disagree with each other. What vocabulary and communicative strategies are used? In what ways and for what reasons might this kind of online group be an appropriate data-collection approach with young people?

CHAPTER 9

Analyzing Data

Photographs get meaning, like all cultural objects, from their context. Even paintings or sculptures, which seem to exist in isolation, hanging on the wall of a museum, get their meaning from a context made up of what has been written about them, either in the label hanging beside them or elsewhere, other visual objects, physically present or just present in viewers' awareness, and from discussions going on around them and around the subject the works are about. If we think there is no context that only means that the maker of the work has cleverly taken advantage of our willingness to provide the context for ourselves.

—BECKER (1998b, p. 88)

Data, whether in the form of transcripts, field notes, maps, drawings, photographs, other documents, or any combination of these, must be made sense of. How do you analyze children's interpretive data, especially when it may entail a mixture of visual, verbal, and textual material? Where do you begin? Although there is an abundance of resources on the use of multiple methods for research with children and youth, there are fewer resources on analysis. This chapter brings together current, interdisciplinary thinking on making sense of visual, verbal, and textual data. We consider the way the analytical process serves to advance the data-collection activity as well as provide a structure for making meaning of complex, dynamic, and varied forms of data.

INTERNAL AND EXTERNAL NARRATIVES OF MEANING

Using multiple modes for communicating experience and meaning is promising as well as challenging. Different data sources provide different data as well as additional information on themes and concepts already shared by the participants. Multiple methods are useful as a means of confirmation and as a way to provide information one data-collection strategy might not have generated. In a study of children's understanding of place, "focus groups, mapping and PhotoVoice provided different yet complementary information about the children's activities—for example, backyard trampolines were often featured in children's photographs but never in mapping or interviews. The role of pets in children's activities was not mentioned in focus groups and could easily have been overlooked" (Darbyshire et al., 2005, p. 424).

All data have what Banks (2001) referred to as internal and external narratives of meaning. The content of an image or text is its internal narrative, or story, whereas the social context in which the data were created is its external narrative. Similarly, "photographs have a double border, the 'frame' in the sense that photographers use the term, to mean what is contained within the viewfinder (and what is selected out), and the 'frame' created by the way we talk about the photograph, particularly in the way we locate it in time as an indicator of memories" (Schratz & Walker, 1995, p. 76). Paying attention to both the internal and external narratives strengthens the analytic reach. Often the ability to make connections is aided by the participants' themselves, for example, in their verbal commentaries on their drawings or photographs. Other times, the researcher situates the data within a conceptual framework to enable a particular commentary or connection.

It is useful to understand how photographers make sense of this meaning-making process. Becker (1998a) looks at the work of photographer Walker Evans in *American Photographs* (Evans, 1938/1988) to consider this question. Drawing from Trachtenberg's (1989) analysis of Evans's work, he shows how Evans used photographs to depict the qualities of American people: their character, beliefs, heroes, pastimes, and work. Evans provides little evidence beyond the 87 photographs displayed one per page. So how is the reader to read these pictures? Many photographers use captions to frame the picture in a specific way; captions point the reader to the important details or themes embedded in a picture. Others, such as Evans, use montage, paying particular attention to how each picture is displayed among other pictures to form a group. Simply put, any image is interpreted within a group of images, building on continuities and discontinuities between images to create a dialogue. Although one picture can leave the viewer uncertain, adding another and another narrows the interpretive field as a coherent story unfolds and a working hypothesis is created. "The image an image follows, the image it precedes, and those even farther away in the sequence of pictures the viewer sees—all those pictures condition our understanding of the picture we are looking at now. The meaning of any one picture arises in its connection with all the others" (Becker, 1998a, p. 5).

The hypothesis the reader creates along the way is tested with each new picture and, in fact, with every new viewing since the multiplicity of connections that could be made leaves open the overall sense that is made of the totality of the data. In this example, the dialogue occurs solely among pictures whose captions mention only their location and the date they were taken. This dialogue could also occur between uncaptioned pictures and an accompanying descriptive text as in Berger and Mohr's book on migrant labor in Europe (Becker, 2002). Alternatively, dialogue is created by chronologically sequencing photographs accompanied by both contextual description and theoretical analysis, as is the case in Mead and Bateson's work on Balinese life (Mead & Bateson, 1942). Much like Banks's internal and external narratives, Becker argues that reading photographs takes time and training and involves both a careful reading of the content and a consideration for how the picture was produced and why. "In such a situation of making and reading photographs, the viewer becomes an active participant, not just the passive recipient of information and ideas constructed by an active author. By selecting the connections to be made from the very many that could be made between the images in any sequence of richly detailed photographs, the viewer constructs the meanings that form the experience of the work" (Becker, 2002, pp. 4–5).

In this way, the internal narrative of any image or document never really gains all of its meaning from its content alone. Even when describing an image, our interpretations do not emerge from the content of the data alone but are embedded in a larger network of purpose and social relationships. From a social constructivist view, data can never directly depict an experience and, therefore, the internal voice of any data source gains meaning from the multiple conditions that brought it into existence and the framework within which we create and compose our own data montage.

Generally, then, data analysis focuses on four areas: (1) the context in which the data were created; (2) the content of the data; (3) the contexts in which and the subjectivities through which the data are interpreted; and (4) the effect or impact of the data on interpreters and readers.

ANALYSIS OF CONTEXT, CONTEXTS OF ANALYSIS

Up until now we have discussed ways in which data are presented either to the researcher for analysis or to the reader of social science reports. But how do we move from a descriptive account of the data we have to work with to an interpretive report of the result of our analytic activity? As we discussed in Chapter 4 and illustrated in Chapters 6 through 8, the data collected from young people will likely include more than the field notes, transcripts, and documents normally encountered in observation and interview studies. Although visual data present special challenges, the overall process of engaging in their analysis provides a guideline for the analysis of any material—visual, verbal, and written. Whatever the dataset, however, one of the first challenges facing qualitative researchers is balancing the views of participants with those of the researcher.

Data do not speak for themselves; data analysis acknowledges the interplay between data and researcher. Sometimes participants seem to agree on something or express a shared perspective. Other times the data have few connecting themes or contradictions are found in the data of one or more participants. Using multiple data sources may increase the likelihood of the latter scenario, but whether there is agreement, inconsistency, or contradiction the researcher bears the responsibility for finding a working hypothesis, perhaps theory, for making sense of these data (Mathison, 1988).

For example, in the following excerpt from a focus group with urban eighth graders, the topic of group work came up. There is little disagreement as students build on each other's responses to form a coherent whole:

RESEARCHER: What kind of activities, or tasks or grouping, do you generally do in the classroom that help you learn? What kinds of things do you like that help you learn?

KYLIE: Being able to pick, when we are told to be in groups, it's better to be able to pick the groups that you are in. It's better than being assigned.

LUKE: Yeah, 'cause when you are assigned a group, a lot of times you get a bunch of people who don't want to work at all and then it's all placed on you.

BLAIR: And a lot of times it's also hard to be like if your teacher assigns you in a group sometimes like if you are good in class they will put you in a group with like people that aren't so good.

BRANDON: Yeah, or they are just a bunch of people that you don't get along with at all so they just don't talk to you at all.

LUKE: But most of the time they let us pick our own groups so that's good.

This passage illustrates how youth in a group interview work together in the co-construction of meaning, but their joint response does not answer the question about whether what they are agreeing about (being able to pick one's own group) actually helps them learn and, if so, how.

In the first interview with the same group, however, disagreement and contradictions arose over how useful the students found the test-taking strategies they learned. In a written response to the question, "Was there a particular test-taking strategy that you were thankful you knew because you needed it on the ELA test? Describe the strategy and why you needed it," Blair wrote, "I was thankful for the chapter titles because it helped you organize your thoughts. For chapter titles you read a paragraph and then name it based on what the paragraph says, you need this because it helps you organize your thoughts and helps you fully understand what you just read." Two other students also wrote responses listing the strategies they were thankful they knew. However, later in our group meeting, when discussing what the students thought of the ELA, Blair contradicts herself:

BLAIR: Like, I knew it was going to be easy, but like everybody was like running around like stressing out about it before and I was like it's so easy, you don't even need as much time. I don't see why they prepare so much for it because how much of the stuff did anybody actually use that we learned in class? Did anybody use all of it?

KYLIE: The chapter titles.

BLAIR: I didn't use the chapter titles. I didn't use anything but I had to write something down.

LUKE: I used a lot of them.

Luke, like most of the other students, goes on to describe the strategies he found useful. Blair reiterates that she found all she had learned "a waste of time."

Data analysis brings together the data, the purpose of the study, and the instincts of the researcher. There is no magic formula. As we mentioned in Chapter 4, analysis begins with our choice of methods, research questions, participants, interview questions, and so on. All of the decisions made along the way have been made with the belief that they would advance our understanding of the topic under inquiry. Keeping a research journal of decisions and ongoing reflections from the beginning of a research study is highly advisable and can help locate shifts in perspective, methodological choices made along the way, and decisions that bear on the quality and content of the data collected. In our study with fourth- and eighth-grade students on their experiences with state standardized testing, before our third and last meeting with the groups, although we felt we had high-quality data on their experiences with testing, we were unsure how much testing would have been part of their conversation about schooling if it had not been for our questions. We decided to have students create timelines of their school year to record the high and low points of being a fourth or eighth grader. This data-collection strategy demonstrated how many nonacademic activities were meaningful to the youth, either as high or low points. Birthdays, field trips, special events like parties, movies or plays, social relationships such as making a new friend, being picked on, and losing a teacher all figured prominently. And there were points of pride, like winning a contest or earning an A. Testing appeared primarily as low points but did not seem to have the significance for the students that we had been attributing to it.

Indigenous and Sensitizing Concepts

Most qualitative research methods textbooks suggest beginning the analysis process by engaging inductively, systematically, and repeatedly with the data.

> A good place to begin inductive analysis is to inventory and define key phrases, terms, and practices that are special to the people in the setting studied. What are the indigenous categories that the people interviewed have created to make sense of their world? What are the practices they engage in that can be understood only within their worldview? Anthropologists call this *emic* analysis and distinguish it from *etic* analysis, which refers to labels imposed by the researcher. (Patton, 2002, p. 454, emphasis in original)

An example of an indigenous concept emerged when discussing stress with the suburban fourth graders and hearing them talk about "warm fuzzies," which turned out to be a stress-reduction practice created by teachers. Because we had not yet conducted the parallel focus group with the urban fourth graders, the emergence of this concept allowed us to explore whether any similar practice was occurring in the other group, whether they called it "warm fuzzies" or not.

Indigenous concepts can also be practices. For example, we noticed that many of the participants used skills they were learning in school to answer written questions that were part of the research process, such as starting their written responses using part of the question. Indigenous concepts can also be a shared representative device, such as seeing the same teacher depicted with a cup of coffee in his hand. Indigenous concepts can be typologies such as the labels they give different peer groups (see Patton, 2002, p. 457).

Inductive analysis often involves in vivo coding, the process of discovering themes, patterns, and indigenous concepts in the data and assigning a code to representative chunks of data. For example, the student responses just presented might have been coded as "in-class group assignments" in the first case and as "test-taking strategies" in the second case. These coded chunks become the building blocks of an emergent theory and can be used to exemplify a specific hypothesis or theoretical notion.

Inductive analysis can also involve focusing on the discursive practices of participants by analyzing the language they use either in their interactions in everyday activities or in the context of interviews. Often used in conjunction with ethnographic studies seeking to understand the culture of a particular group and the group's communicative rules and patterns of behavior, sociolinguistic analysis or other forms of conversational analysis can provide a lens through which to analyze individual and group interview data. This kind of analysis "involves first examining the communicative structure of the interview as a whole, so that the meanings of specific responses are considered in regard to the whole event" (Eder & Fingerson, 2003, p. 46). When considering the two eighth-grade interview examples presented earlier from this perspective, we notice that Blair often brings a negative spin to the discussion or contradicts her peers, whereas Luke brings an agreeable tone and is often heard presenting a more supportive picture of school practices. Although there is no reason to discount these perspectives as not being these students' accurate portrayals of their perspectives and opinions, this kind of analysis can assist in understanding existing peer dynamics and relationships that play a part in how experience is presented and constructed in the social context of an interview.

Inductive analysis works from specific instances to generalizations, theoretical connections, or explanations. In contrast, deductive analysis involves analyzing the data using existing theoretical or guiding frameworks. Although many qualitative analysts talk of "emergent" themes, most analysts understand that, even while these themes are grounded in the data, they have emerged through the researcher's interaction with the data. "The idea persists that categories should (will?) emerge from the data. My experience is that they cannot do it on their own. As author-researcher, you must go to their rescue or they will perish" (Wolcott, 1994, p. 63). Good social constructivist data analysis requires both inductive and deductive perspectives as well as abductive reasoning, which combines the deductive reasoning of generating hypotheses and testing them and the inductive process of theory construction in a back-and-forth movement between data, theory, and the purpose and focus of the research.

One way of moving between theory and data in the construction of meaning is to use sensitizing concepts that help organize indigenous themes to relate them to the research questions. Unlike indigenous concepts, sensitizing concepts are analytic categories the researcher brings to the data and are typically derived from existing theories or related literature (Patton, 2002). In the interview excerpt presented previously, our focus on the role of stress to motivate and constrain action is an example of a sensitizing concept.

Analysis Creates Its Own Narrative: The Research Story

Analysis involves organizing the data for interpretation, and in so doing the analysis begins the creation of a new narrative: the interpretive report. Blanchet-Cohen et al.'s (2003) study of children's experience and understanding of environmental issues illustrates this interplay. During an environmental conference, 400 adolescents (10- and 12-year-olds) were invited to share their perspectives on the environment, and the researchers engaged small groups of children in several map-making processes around a variety of environmental themes. One of the maps was an outline of a participant's body used by the rest of the group to share their ideas, in words or images, using the inside and outside of the figure as an organizational device. Faced with a large number of such maps, Blanchet-Cohen et al. used a small group of the child participants as analysts. They focused on how the data helped them understand how children viewed "environmental action as it relates to themselves and their communities." To do so, they created a coding scheme to apply to the data contained in the map, a process that was both labor intensive and challenging.

> For instance, it was impossible to code the group maps in a way that differentiated the ideas of one author from another. Too often, it was difficult to determine the beginning and end of a statement, and whether or not the whole statement was made by the same author. To overcome this challenge, we decided that each new idea would be coded separately, regardless of the author. We also agreed that both visual and written statements would be coded the same way. For example, we coded a graphic with a stop sign under the "Stop doing" category, in the same way that we would code a statement with the word "stop" in it. Once we determined the boundaries of the phrase or drawing, we had to code the item in its context. To focus on a single keyword or segment of a graph would have been misleading. For example, if a

child wrote or drew the symbol for "reduce reuse recycle," we considered it as a directive for an overall attitude change, hence a "Value" statement. However, we considered statements such as "reuse sheets of paper, reduce plastic," as calls for personal behavioural change, and hence fell under the "Choice" category. We attempted to consistently code the overall meaning provided by the group of words or drawings. For cross-verification, different researchers verified the coding. (Blanchet-Cohen et al., 2003).

We include this example to illustrate the decisions that are made and to highlight that analysis can seldom be approached in a predetermined way. Analysis consists of a careful reading and rereading of the data, an inventory of the content of the data, an examination of the contexts—personal, interpersonal, and situational—that inform the construction of meaning, and the stance of the researcher. All of these affect the construction of meaning from beginning to end.

> An interview [or any other form of expression, whether written, verbal, or visual] cannot be seen as an expression of the interviewee's own "authentic voice," but as generated through such "filters" as the participants' perceptions of the situation, the research focus, interview questions, likely audience and interpretation, as well as the structural constraints they face and their personal values and biographies. (Alldred & Burman, 2005, p. 181)

ANALYZING VISUAL DATA

Researchers working with visual material often ask whether it is possible or advisable to interpret a drawing or photograph from the content of the drawing or photograph itself. As we discussed in Chapter 7, visual forms of expression are different from verbal forms and present meaning to the audience in different ways. It necessarily follows that analysis of images presents its own unique challenges.

A drawing or photograph evokes a different kind of response and is favored for its immediacy and accessibility.

> Aesthetic expression confers on what it expresses an existence in itself, installs it in nature as a thing perceived and accessible to all, or conversely plucks the signs themselves—the person of the actor, or the color and canvas of the painter—from their empirical existence and bears them off into another world. No one will deny that here the pro-

cess of expression brings the meaning into being or makes it effective, and does not merely translate it. (Merleau-Ponty, 1962, p. 183)

The picture "stands alone," as it were, in the immediacy of its presence. Images have a way of maintaining the present tense and so are powerful ways to represent events, people, and meaning as if they were still happening (Schratz & Walker, 1995).

The drawings in Figures 9.1 and 9.2 are the result of asking fourth graders to remember how they felt taking the ELA test and to draw themselves feeling that feeling. Vincent, a Native/African American, and Joseph, a Hispanic, drew these self-portraits. Both boys attended a kindergarten–fifth grade urban elementary school in a poor, multicultural neighborhood in upstate New York.

There is much in these drawings that evokes meaning. Vincent depicts himself sitting at a desk. The desk comes up to his chest so that he seems small in comparison. He sits with legs together, eyes

FIGURE 9.1. Vincent's self-portrait.

FIGURE 9.2. Joseph's self-portrait.

shut. Around his body is a shaky line. A line coming out of his head looks as if there was an attempt to erase it. Finally, in bold, large letters, the word "ELA" is drawn above him, with each letter the size of Vincent himself. Whereas Vincent sits a small, tightly drawn body in blue under big blue letters, Joseph's picture is noticeable for its color and movement. His body, drawn in blue, is made up of free-flowing circular scribbles. His face looks straight at us: a tense smile and eyes framed by large black-rimmed glasses. A dark green cap sits on his head. His arm, which lies across a bright red-orange desk on which lies a rectangle with the letters "ELA" written on it, seems super-sized and his large hand (also blue) holds a blue pencil, standing straight up, as wide and tall as he himself. Tracing the outline of this figure, desk, and pencil are jagged colored lines, red, black, pink, and orange. They all sit on layers of color. Above them are the letters "ELa" in light blue and yellow, softer colors not found in the rest of the drawing.

We can feel Vincent's sense of powerlessness just as we can sense Joseph's intensity and sense of self. We do not need more information to come to these interpretations. These pictures evoke a response, and they make sense to us. We can understand images without being told anything about them. That does not mean, however, that this understanding is useful, meaningful, or close to what the creator was attempting to convey to us about his or her experience. "When creative or artistic works are produced not as an exercise in 'spontaneous' self-expression, but rather because a researcher has *requested* that they be made, questions about the interpretation of such work seem especially poignant" (Gauntlett, 2005, emphasis in original). Although these drawings are meaningful on their own, no data can ever stand alone. We know much about the context within which the drawings were acquired; thus, we are already reading these drawings from the outside in, from the perspective of "the way I was feeling taking the ELA."

Generally, there has been as much mistrust in the reliability of images to depict social reality as there has been trust in the use of words to do so (Schratz & Walker, 1995). Both modes of expression, however, have the same dilemma: mediating between lived experience and representing the meaning of that experience. Both offer different strengths. A verbal sentence may have multiple meanings: the way the words are put together within a sequence of dialogue, the intonation and facial expression of the speaker, and the content of the statement all serve to assist with its interpretation. Images also express intonation and feeling. There is a living quality to images that is often absent in verbal statements. What is lacking, however, is a road map, a way around the details of the drawing, what they mean, and what they convey.

Most researchers using children's images caution against interpreting the drawings independently of having witnessed the students creating them or without attached commentary. In these situations, the researcher resorts to creating and using a coding matrix that catalogues the content of the drawings so that they can then be organized around particular themes (see, e.g., Wheelock et al., 2000). Whether the researcher is present or not at the time the drawing is made, a visual depiction of an experience reveals questions that cannot be answered without further information. For example, one of the drawings collected by Wheelock et al. (2000) depicted a teacher with his pants on fire. Was this wishful thinking, an actual event, or to be taken metaphorically? After consulting with a teacher, they found out that this was an actual event when a teacher accidentally lit a match against some change in his pocket. Written and spoken languages push people to present their stories in a coherent order in a way that an image doesn't require, making images more ambiguous.

> If we are looking at visual material in the hope of ascertaining how the artist/producer feels about something, this *is* more difficult than if we are faced with a verbal statement where a person *says* how they feel about something. Interpreting the latter is not necessarily straightforward either, but the researcher has something clear, intentional, and *verifiable,* to go on. (Gauntlett, 2005, emphasis in original)

When seeking to understand any material produced by participants, it is helpful to ask the participants themselves about the meaning of the material. Returning to Vincent and Joseph's self-portraits, we can add captions based on interviewing the students about their drawings and their experience taking the ELA. Vincent mentioned that taking the ELA was "scary," but other than that he was not particularly talkative. Joseph, on the other hand, articulated that it was not that he was scared but that he was "worried, 'cause if I don't, if I fail again, 'cause I did third grade, 'cause in third grade my teacher, I was in Manhattan and my teacher said 'Some of you aren't going to pass into fourth grade and I didn't.' If he passed me, the fourth grade, I would have been in fifth grade."

The addition of verbal commentary, even when consisting of only one word, helps stabilize the meaning of the image (Gauntlett, 2005). It provides a road map into understanding the feeling and experience depicted. Figure 9.3 summarizes a framework for analyzing images as data. An image can be read in a number of ways, and depending on the purpose of the research, some or all of the readings referred to in Figure 9.3 might be helpful.

	Focus of analysis		Analysis questions
Focus on subject matter	Literal reading	Low inference ▲ High	What are the physical features of the image? Who or what is portrayed? What is the setting?
	Biographical reading		What is the relationship of the image to current practices? To identities? How is the image socially situated?
	Empathetic reading		What common experiences are invoked?
	Iconic reading		How does the image relate to bigger ideas, values, events, cultural constructions?
	Psychological reading		What are the intended states of mind and being?
Focus on image creation	Technical reading		What are the design features? Are images scaled or mapped?
	Editorial reading		What values and knowledge are communicated by the author or creator?
	Indexical reading		How does the image relate to values of the time and place?
	Spectatorship reading		Where is the viewer situated in relation to the image?
Focus on audience/ viewers	Reading of effects		What impact does the image have on viewers?
	Reflexive reading		How do viewers see themselves within the interpretation? How does the image interact with biography?

FIGURE 9.3. Framework for analyzing visual data.

ANALYSIS GOES ON AND ON

Analysis is an ongoing process. It begins by critically analyzing the assumptions that are embedded in our questions, by listening deeply to how children respond to and understand these questions, and by continuously considering the way our interactions, questions, and methods are contributing to the breadth and depth of the knowledge shared by the children. Because language can take on multiple forms of significance and children may or may not have the same resources as an adult participant to ask for clarification or for a rewording of the question, the researcher must also listen carefully for these occurrences of misunderstanding. This ability involves more than comprehension. It involves the ability to consider whether the misunderstanding is one of meaning or one of perspective. In other words, is the question relevant to a 9-year-old facing daily test-prep activities in an urban classroom, or is it only relevant to a 40-something researcher with an abstract interest in the way testing interfaces with societal structures? Although there is no one best way to go about analyzing data, we provide some guiding points, relevant for all data, visual, verbal, or textual:

1. What is the context(s) in which the data were produced? Context includes interpersonal relationships and cultural and social constructions. Context also includes the quality of the research (e.g., the questions asked).

2. What is the content of the data? This may include some form of frequency, thematic or content analysis, coding, or other organizational schema.

3. What are the contexts in which and subjectivities through which the data are viewed? This includes the researcher's as well as participants' subjectivities. For example, it is clear on reading the transcript that Vincent was not aware that he would have to share his drawing and so is clearly taken aback when he was done drawing to find this out. He points out that taking the ELA was "scary," but this was in the context of discussing Joseph's drawing. When asked about his drawing directly, he gives two responses, one unintelligible and the other simply a shrug, and then he responds to the question, "Did you feel differently than Joseph in his picture, because your pic-

tures are quite a bit different?" by stating, "'Cause I don't know how to draw. I don't like drawing. I just like building." Vincent did find taking the ELA scary; this is evident in many of his other responses about the tests. What is less clear is his relationship to his drawing or drawing in general and what we as researchers are to make of statements about the medium, whether it is drawing, talking, or writing. Does it matter whether a participant likes or dislikes a medium in terms of how we are to interpret it?

4. How is agency of the data to be considered in analysis? Along with how one's preconceived perspectives shape how we view certain participants, ideas, or data, data have their own magnetism. We are drawn to images that evoke a strong reaction or verbal statements that articulate clearly or perhaps poetically the expressed viewpoint. Being aware of how the presentation of the data influences its analysis is also important.

Just as documentary photographers display meaning through the interplay among photographs, narrative texts, and viewers, social constructivist data analysis creates a similar montage, a dance of meaning as data and theory are revealed to readers/viewers, leading them to new kinds and forms of understanding.

DISCUSSION QUESTIONS

1. Write a memo about what you can say about the data you have collected thus far. Consider what you feel you are beginning to know about the topic and how different themes are related. From this assessment, develop a series of questions to explore through further data collection.

2. Broaden your views on analysis by choosing to research a specific approach (phenomenology, narrative, discourse analysis, analysis of visual material, multimodal analysis of videotaping). Do a quick review of the literature on the approach and find at least three studies that are using this analytic approach in their work with children. What kinds of questions are these studies looking to explore? What kinds of data-collection activities did they conduct? What were the strengths and weaknesses of the analysis?

CHAPTER 10

Children as Researchers

The study of kids remains fundamentally a practice
of reconstructing their experiences within the
disciplinary and discursive concerns of adults.
—NESPOR (1998, p. 370)

Eliciting children's perspectives and involving children in research
is a necessary element of inclusive, empowering, and socially just
research designs. However, eliciting children's perspectives in adult-
designed studies rarely reflects children's interests and, unless young
people participate in designing the study, may not be empowering
or relevant to their lives. This chapter focuses on the theoretical and
empirical reasons why some researchers are moving toward a more
collaborative research relationship with children. More specifically,
this chapter questions the taken-for-granted notion that involving
children in research, whether as participants or designers, necessarily improves the validity of findings or benefits the youth involved.
Although we argue throughout this book that the current attention
researchers are paying to the kinds of relationships and research
contexts they are developing with children is good, justified, and
necessary, it does not follow that recruiting child participants in
adult-designed studies and topics is necessarily bad or less valid than
participatory studies.

There is a tendency in the literature on children-as-researchers to dismiss studies designed by adults with children as exploitative or oppressive. Children, like adults, can benefit or be harmed by taking part in research experiences. Inviting children to talk about and share their experiences on a topic of the researcher's choice may provide a social context that enriches their lives in unexpected ways. Inviting children to develop and design their own research agendas will promote different experiences and outcomes than those fostered by researcher-led designs. The success or failure of one or the other is more than a matter of methods and involves careful attention to all aspects of the research design and researcher–participant relationship. Our intent here is not to provide an overview of the role children have undertaken as researchers and co-researchers. Rather, we want to unravel some of the questions and issues raised by researchers interested in involving children in all aspects of a research study. First, we provide a brief overview of different forms of youth–adult partnerships, with examples of these partnerships. Then we describe reasons for involving youth as co-researchers. Finally, we conclude with questions to consider when involving children as researchers.

THE POWER OF CHILDREN'S VOICES

There is a deep relationship between who controls the production of knowledge and who holds the power in a society (Delgado, 2006). The push to seek out the voices of children in research on and about children comes from a variety of disciplines and practices. However, seeking out children's voices is only one form of inclusion when it comes to engaging children in research. Figure 10.1 illustrates a continuum of possibilities for youth–adult research partnerships.

Adult-centered leadership is the most common adult–youth relationship, characterized by adult researchers leading and youth participating in the adult-designed research tasks. This book focuses primarily on this research relationship between adults and young people. Adult-led collaboration involves youth participants making limited decisions about some aspects of the research design or its activities. This approach, similar to the first, continues to place adults in charge but allows young people to make some decisions. For example, Thomas and O'Kane (1998) gave their young

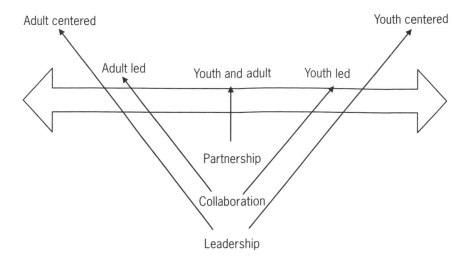

FIGURE 10.1. Youth–adult research partnership continuum. Based on Jones and Perkins (2002).

participants the opportunity to choose the location for interviews, whether they wanted to be interviewed alone or with someone else, and which group activities they wished to participate in. In another example, Alvermann et al. (1996) involved young people in interpreting the data, thus taking advantage of their insider knowledge. The students viewed, reflected on, interpreted, and explained what was going on during classroom discussions while viewing videotaped discussions.

Youth–adult research partnerships are designed to give adults and youth equal opportunities to make decisions about the design and conduct of the research study. For example, Oldfather (1995), in her longitudinal study of students' views of learning and motivation, created multiple partnerships with students through helping with data interpretation, participating in conference presentations, and eventually leading studies of their own. Although initially the students did not collect data, "they were involved in identifying critical issues and questions that we pursued" (p. 132). Once in high school, these same students initiated their own research projects and collaborated with teachers to continue to study motivation from the students' and teachers' perspectives. What started as an adult–youth partnership evolved into a youth-led collaboration.

Nespor's (1998) ethnographic study of an urban elementary school gave students an active role and exemplifies the youth-led collaboration approach.

> When a fourth-grade teacher asked me to supervise a student newsletter, I took the opportunity to encourage kids to create stories based on investigative research. I let them use my tape recorder for interviews, which I then transcribed, inserting pseudonyms, and returned. Their teacher and I and their classmates then helped the reporters/researchers craft their data into newsletter articles. (p. 378)

Engaging students in research or turning the research process over to young people involves negotiation, communication, and a willingness to give them the reins even when their destination is not clear. How and why young people go about conducting research is as important to understanding their cultural worlds as learning what they find. Nespor shares several stories of how students took control of research issues and instruments, arguing for certain items to be taken off of survey instruments and dismissing Nespor's suggested topics as "grown-up stuff," offering instead that they research topics of interest to students such as "How to get your parents to do what you want" (p. 379). Nespor found that, given space, children had their own ideas of what research was for. Over time the students in this study developed their own agendas for using research practices: conducting multiple interviews to construct a collective complaint for something that they did not like, such as getting parents' signatures on their homework folders. In this way, student researchers did not necessarily develop new knowledge. What they did instead was use the process of knowledge generation and synthesis to gather existing students' experiences and understandings in support of an activist's agenda for change.

In an evaluation of an academically accelerated middle-school program, Mathison encouraged the youth to participate in the inquiry and suggested a number of questions and methods they might consider. This being a precocious, committed group of students, she thought creative strategies like drawing, storytelling, and poetry writing about what the students thought was valuable and problematic about the program would be appealing. The students, however, wanted to interview alumni of the program, a traditional research method but one that was based on their needs and interests. The students knew they were better positioned to find and contact alumni (through family, friends, neighbors), often spoke the same first language as other students, and were keenly interested in what the program experience might mean for their future (Would they get into the best college? What kind of jobs would they get?). The students co-opted the research process to explore their futures rather than to describe their present lives.

Not all young people, given the chance, will use research in the same way. Creating opportunities for young people to take charge of research requires letting go of adult predetermined notions of what counts as research. Youth-centered leadership research practice puts youth in charge with limited or no adult supervision or collaboration. Given the power inequalities between children and adults, finding examples of this type of research necessitates going outside normal venues for dissemination of research findings. Youth-centered leadership can be found in research on sustainable development, community and socially oriented activist projects, and environmental and global awareness projects developed and run by youth around the world. For example, What Kids Can Do (WKCD) is a nonprofit organization created to foster youth-led knowledge creation that contributes to policy debates about school, society, and world affairs. WKCD's website, *www.whatkidscando.org/*, describes many such projects, ones that spring from youth interests, motivations, and strengths and exploit many forms of data collection and representation, especially the use of multimedia.

WHY PARTNER WITH YOUNG PEOPLE?

Involving youth in research is not a new idea. Teachers using inquiry-based learning have routinely involved young people in the development of inquiry tools and researchable questions, collecting data, and the analysis and writing up of the findings. Sometimes this is done within the classroom, sometimes the project focuses on a whole school, and other times children conduct community-based or oral history projects. The methods, therefore, are rarely foreign to children. Community development and service learning projects also actively involve children as consultants, active participants, and as co-researchers, and there are a growing number of youth-developed websites that communicate their work as independent leaders and researchers. The development of a broader vision of including young people has roots in action research, participatory evaluation, community development, global concerns about the well-being and health of young people, and the changing conceptions of the sociology of childhood. Furthermore, the 1989 United Nations Convention on the Rights of the Child continues to alter the way children around the world are participating in decision making on topics and practices that affect their lives. Youth involvement in research and evaluation goes by many names: "students-as-researchers, voiced research, peer research, youth-run research, participatory research, participatory action research, empowerment research" (Delgado, 2006, p. 17). What holds them together is the importance of "participation, decision-making, and action."

More and more youth are invited to sit on school and community boards and participate in political decision-making processes (Sinclair, 2004; Tisdall & Davis, 2004). They also actively protest so their voices are heard (Badham, 2004). These efforts help pave the way for youth as researchers. "Youth-led research, youth participation, and youth development, for example, best capture the goals of engaging youth in initiatives that effectively transform not only them but also their community in the process" (Delgado, 2006, p. 5). Nevertheless, actively involving youth in decisions affecting social research is evolving slowly. Youth involvement efforts range from being pedagogical (i.e., teaching students research skills) to being a crucial element of community change. For example, classroom-based action research in British (and American) schools is widespread but underpublished and not valued as academic research (Alderson, 2000). On the other hand, children are seen as making valuable contributions to change in developing countries. The literacy skills taught in schools are making schools centers of health and development research, with children leading the way (Alderson, 2000). However, "the danger of such collaborations is that they can easily turn into forms of internal colonization in which we merely train kids to formulate themselves and their problems in our terms to answer our questions. This is a special risk if we use collaborative research simply to learn more about kids instead of taking it as an opportunity to study with them the world we have in common" (Nespor, 1998, p. 383).

Authentic collaboration involves authentic relationships in which partners learn about each other and each other's worlds in the process of working together on shared interests. Youth-led research is premised on five beliefs:

1. Youth have abilities that can be tapped in developing and implementing a research project.

2. Youth bring to a research project a unique perspective or voice that cannot but help the process of answering questions about youth.

3. Youth are vital stakeholders in the process and outcome of research.

4. The knowledge and skills youth acquire through active participation in research can transfer to other aspects of their lives.

5. Youth-led research can help broaden and revitalize an activity that has a reputation as being boring, inconsequential, and of interest to only a small select group of adults. (Delgado, 2006, p. 19)

To understand the contributions young people make to social science research, it helps to consider the reasons why children have been dismissed as participants, co-researchers, or researchers in their own right. The belief that young people do not have enough experience, knowledge, or skill has kept many researchers from seeing children as co-researchers or even competent informants (Kellett, Forrest, Dent, & Ward, 2004). Delgado (2006, p. 32) lists reasons why adults may not include youth in research or think of them as incapable of being researchers:

1. Lack of interest in or disdain for the input given by children and youth

2. Lack of confidence in youth's experience and expertise

3. Differences in how youth and adults live their lives

4. Stereotypes of youth

5. Lack of understanding how youth process information, especially at different ages

6. Involving youth is labor intensive and therefore expensive

7. Fear that empowerment of youth will disempower adults

8. Need for skills to address differences of opinions and potential conflicts among youth

9. Inertia or resistance to change in social roles and relationships

10. Time needed to shift to a paradigm within which youth are in decision-making positions.

Most of these reasons focus on the competence or willingness of individuals, children or adults, but social and structural factors lead also to the exclusion and disempowerment of youth in research practices.

> To move toward more fully authorizing the perspectives of students is not simply to include them in existing conversations within existing power structures. Authorizing student perspectives means ensuring that there are legitimate and valued spaces within which students can speak, re-tuning our ears so that we can hear what they say, and redirecting our actions in response to what we hear. (Cook-Sather, 2002, p. 4)

To authorize the perspectives and voices of young people requires more than inclusion, it involves a commitment to including them in the development and design of the very social institutions researchers study.

THE POSSIBILITY OF *TRUE* PARTNERSHIPS

We cannot take seriously our position on the essentialness of including children's voices without considering how their voices are included. What inclusion and participation strategies are being used? How do these strategies contribute to altering the power balance between adults and young people? What can we do better? Children are being acknowledged as important stakeholders in evaluation (Sabo, 2003) and participants in research (Delgado, 2006), yet inquiry is still primarily designed by adults. Is it because it is an adult conception? Is it because when it is conducted solely by youth and for youth we don't recognize it as research, especially since it is rarely published in scholarly journals? Is it because we lack the imagination to allow young people to shape our work? Collaborating with young co-researchers certainly raises important ethical issues regarding power and voice.

In a practice shaped by adults and applied in adult-developed institutions, creating authentic structural changes that alter youth's societal roles, thus giving them control over what counts as research, is difficult. Involving young people as co-researchers can develop "epistemological empowerment," a sense of agency and intellectual know-how when one is involved in an active and critical process of constructing meaning (Oldfather, 1995; Oldfather & Dahl, 1994).

It also implies learning that knowledge is socially constructed and, therefore, can be re-constructed anew.

Engaging young people as research collaborators or encouraging their own research agendas, therefore, involves a reconfiguration of the research relationship as well as an awareness of the political consequences in particular settings. However, can we ever create truly democratic or equal relationships when working with children as co-researchers? One necessary element is a critical self-reflective stance on the part of the adult researchers.

> Critical reflective practice in studies that involve children as researchers includes analysis of "adult"-self as researcher, scrutiny of theory and assumptions and the capacity to be within, part of and at the same time reflect on the dynamics of interactions within which one engages children. Reflection must be both *precursor* to children's involvement (examination of own behaviour, values and role) and also *concurrent* with children's involvement (examination of the research process as it unfolds). Critical reflective practice provides opportunities for learning and growth and helps to avoid the inadvertent exploitation or coercion of children. (A. Jones, 2004, p. 115)

Critical reflection in research with children focuses on (1) the context within which young people will be sought out as co-researchers, including possible barriers or supports for the work that will be undertaken; (2) the process of gaining access, consent, and permission and how these will be negotiated and with whom; (3) procedures for negotiating roles and responsibilities; (4) issues of safety if children are going to seek out contact with individuals or groups (whether these contacts are within an institutional setting or outside of it); and (5) the methods for carrying out the research and how much time young people will devote to the project and whether they will be paid for it (Alderson, 2000; A. Jones, 2004).

Research is always political. It is a form of participation in social discourses in how research is conducted, with whom, and about what, and participation in research necessarily shapes how people and knowledge are reproduced in society. Therefore, it is important to strive for inclusion of all voices in social science research. We advocate for youth leadership roles in all aspects of social science research design, collection, and interpretation. Nevertheless, we should also strive for more active roles in other research partnerships with children and youth. Simply adding young people to the research team is not enough to prevent distortions of children's views, exploitation, or oppression (Alderson, 2000). Indeed, we have much to learn about the impact of research partnerships with children, including how to situate the knowledge constructed in such partnerships. For example, Boocock (1981) trained and paid 10- to 12-year-old kids to interview similar-age children on their daily routines, and adults interviewed the other half of the participants. Comparing the results, she found that children reported more deviant behavior to child interviewers than to adults. In another study, African American first-grade girls interpreted videotape data of themselves at school and found that their interpretations differed dramatically from those of the researchers and their teachers (Boocock & Scott, 2005). There is much to be learned about young people's worlds and viewpoints, and our own, when we provide opportunities for the two to work side by side. We do not assume that empowerment occurs only if young people have autonomous control of the research design and process, and researchers have much to learn by developing multiple ways of including and involving youth in authentic and empowering ways.

Research partnerships with youth require specific strategies that level the playing field for adults and youth and create a shared research agenda. The decision to engage youth precedes the determination about what the research questions are and how they might be answered. Research workshops, boot camps, or institutes are a key strategy for bringing the research collaborators together to collectively define research questions, identify and learn about data collection techniques (many of which have been described in this book, like, e.g., art, photography, interviewing, observation, oral histories), and consider what the products and outcomes of the research might be (e.g., articles, conference presentations, websites, performances, poetry, exhibits, brochures). This workshop approach might involve reading relevant theories or research together (exploring the role of, e.g., age, race, gender, class, and sexuality in social life), considering cultural materials relevant to participants (like listening to hip-hop music or exploring youth-centered websites), and learning how to use particular research skills (like photography or interviewing skills). (See D. Morgan et al., 2004, for an example of a youth researcher summer institute that culminated in a youth-led research project on hustling.) This approach to design, not just the doing of the research, gives youth a genuine opportunity to not simply fit into the practice of research as adult researchers know it but to engage in the reformation of that practice so the research speaks directly to youth issues and youth worldviews.

As discussed in Chapter 5, social constructivist research, whether positioning children as participants or co-researchers, involves the construction of relationships, and the relational nature of the situation opens up new ethical dilemmas. Engaging young people as participants or co-researchers is more than a project: It is a way of repositioning the voices of young people and of sharing inquiry and understanding of each other's worlds. As participants in a shared social world, young people, whatever their age, situation, or social position, should be seen and treated as essential actors in that world. We have much to learn from sharing the design, collection of data, and interpretation processes with young people, and our world has much to gain.

DISCUSSION QUESTIONS

1. Locate a research study in which young people were active co-researchers. Describe what the study was about, how the young people were recruited, what kind of decisions were turned over to the young people, which ones were retained by adult collaborators, and what was done to collect, analyze, and report the information.

2. Brainstorm with some young people about research and what they, if given the opportunity, would seek to find out about themselves, others, or events in the world. Were you surprised by their responses in any way? Did their responses confirm your assumptions or make you think differently about how young people might respond to your interest area? If so, how?

References

Abel, E. L., & Buckley, B. E. (1977). *The handwriting on the wall: Towards a sociology and psychology of graffiti.* Westport, CT: Greenwood Press.

Adler, L. L. (1982). Children's drawings as an indicator of individual preferences reflecting group values: A programmatic study. In L. L. Adler (Ed.), *Cross-cultural research at issue* (pp. 71–98). New York: Academic Press.

Adler, P. A., & Adler, P. (1998). *Peer power: Preadolescent culture and identity.* New Brunswick, NJ: Rutgers University Press.

Alanen, L., & Mayall, B. (2001). *Conceptualizing child–adult relations.* New York: Routledge/Falmer.

Alderson, P. (1993). *Children's consent to surgery.* Buckingham, UK: Open University Press.

Alderson, P. (1995). *Researching with children: Children, ethics and social research.* London: Save the Children.

Alderson, P. (2000). *Young children's rights: Exploring beliefs, attitudes, principles and practice.* Philadelphia: Jessica Kingsley.

Alderson, P. (2004). Ethics. In S. Fraser, V. Lewis, S. Ding, M. Kellett, & C. Robinson (Eds.), *Doing research with children and young people* (pp. 97–112). Thousand Oaks, CA: Sage.

Alderson, P. (2005). Designing ethical research with children. In A. Farrell (Ed.), *Ethical research with children* (pp. 27–36). New York: Open University Press.

Alland, J. A. (1983). *Playing with form: Children draw in six cultures.* New York: Columbia University Press.

Alldred, P., & Burman, E. (2005). Analyzing children's accounts using discourse analysis. In S. Greene & D. Hogan (Eds.), *Researching children's experience: Approaches and methods* (pp. 175–198). London: Sage.

Alvermann, D. E., Young, J. P., Weaver, D., Hinchman, K. A., Moore, D. W., & Phelps, S. F. (1996). Middle and high school students' perceptions of how they experience text-based discussions: A multicase study. *Reading Research Quarterly, 31*(3), 244–267.

Astor, R. A., Meyer, H. A., & Behre, W. J. (1999). Unowned places and times: Maps and interviews about violence in high schools. *American Educational Research Journal, 36*(1), 3–42.

Badham, B. (2004). Participation—for a change: Disabled young people lead the way. *Children and Society, 18,* 143–154.

Ball, S. (1985). Participant observation with pupils. In R. G. Burgess (Ed.), *Strategies of educational research: Qualitative methods* (pp. 23–53). Philadelphia: Falmer Press.

Banks, M. (2001). *Visual methods in social research.* London: Sage.

Barker, J., & Weller, S. (2003). "Never work with children?" The geography of methodological issues in research with children. *Qualitative Research, 3*(2), 207–227.

Becker, H. S. (1967). Whose side are we on? *Social Problems, 14,* 239–247.

Becker, H. S. (1998a). Categories and comparisons: How we find meaning in photographs. *Visual Anthropology Review, 14*(2), 3–10.

Becker, H. S. (1998b). Visual sociology, documentary photography and photojournalism: It's (almost) all a matter of context. In J. Prosser (Ed.), *Image-based research: A sourcebook for qualitative researchers* (pp. 84–96). London: Falmer Press.

Becker, H. S. (2002). Visual evidence: A seventh man, the specified generalization, and the work of the reader. *Visual Studies, 17*(1), 3–11.

Belmont Report. (1979). *Ethical principles and guidelines for the protection of human subjects of research.* Washington, DC: U.S. Department of Health, Education and Welfare. Retrieved May 16, 2007, from *www.hhs.gov/ohrp/humansubjects/guidance/belmont.htm*.

Blanchet-Cohen, N., Ragan, D., & Amsden, J. (2003). Children becoming social actors: Using visual maps to understand children's views of environmental change. *Children, Youth and Environments, 13.* Retrieved July 10, 2006, from *www.colorado.edu/journals/cye/13_2/FieldReports/Mapping/Mapping.htm*.

Blaut, J. M., Stea, D., Spencer, C., & Blades, M. (2003). Mapping as a cultural and cognitive universal. *Annals of the Association of American Geographers, 93*(1), 165–185.

Blumenreich, M. (2004). Avoiding the pitfalls of "conventional" narrative research: Using poststructural theory to guide the creation of narratives of children with HIV. *Qualitative Research, 4*(1), 77–90.

Bogolub, E. B., & Thomas, N. (2005). Parental consent and the ethics of research with foster children: Beginning a cross-cultural dialogue. *Qualitative Social Work, 4*(3), 271–292.

Boocock, S. S. (1981). The life space of children. In S. Keller (Ed.), *Building for women* (pp. 93–116). Lexington, MA: Lexington Books.

Boocock, S. S., & Scott, K. A. (2005). *Kids in context: The sociological study of children and childhoods.* New York: Rowman & Littlefield.

Brooker, L. (2001). Interviewing children. In G. M. Naughton, S. A. Rolfe, & I. Siraj-Blatchford (Eds.), *Doing early childhood research: International perspectives on theory and practice* (pp. 163–177). Philadelphia: Open University Press.

Cappello, M. (2005). Photo interviews: Eliciting data through conversations with children. *Field Methods, 17*(2), 170–182.

Caputo, V. (1995). Anthropology's silent "others": A consideration of some of the methodological issues for the study of youth and children's cultures. In V. Amit-Talai & H. Wulff (Eds.), *Youth cultures: A cross-cultural perspective* (pp. 19–42). New York: Routledge.

Carter, P. L. (2005). *Keepin' it real: School success beyond black and white.* New York: Oxford University Press.

Chaplin, E. (1994). *Sociology and visual representation.* New York: Routledge.

Christensen, P., & Prout, A. (2002). Working with ethical symmetry in social research with children. *Childhood, 9*(4), 477–497.

Christensen, P., & Prout, A. (2005). Anthropological and sociological perspectives on the study of children. In S. Greene & D. Hogan (Eds.), *Researching children's experience: Approaches and methods* (pp. 42–60). London: Sage.

Clark, A. (2004). The mosaic approach and research with young children. In V. Lewis, M. Kellett, C. Robinson, S. Fraser, & S. Ding (Eds.), *The reality of research with children and young people* (pp. 142–161). Thousand Oaks, CA: Sage.

Clark, A., & Moss, P. (2001). *Listening to young children: The mosaic approach.* London: National Children's Bureau.

Coles, M. (1996). The magicfying glass: What we know of children talk in the early years. In N. Hall & J. Martello (Eds.), *Listening to children think: Exploring talk in the early years* (pp. 1–17). London: Hodder & Stoughton.

Collier, J., Jr. (1957). Photography in anthropology: A report on two experiments. *American Anthropologist, 59,* 843–859.

Collier, J., Jr., & Collier, M. (1986). *Visual anthropology: Photography as a research method.* Albuquerque: University of New Mexico Press.

Cook-Sather, A. (2002). Authorizing students' perspectives: Toward trust, dialogue, and change in education. *Educational Researcher, 31*(4), 3–14.

Corsaro, W. A. (1981). Entering the child's world: Research strategies for field entry and data collection in a preschool setting. In J. L. Green & C. Wallat (Eds.), *Ethnography and language in educational settings* (pp. 117–146). Norwood, NJ: Ablex.

Corsaro, W. A. (1996). Transitions in early childhood: The promise of comparative, longitudinal ethnography. In R. Jessor, A. Colby, & R. Shweder (Eds.), *Ethnography and human development* (pp. 419–457). Chicago: University of Chicago Press.

Corsaro, W. A. (2003). *"We're friends right?" Inside kids' culture.* Washington, DC: Joseph Henry Press.

Corsaro, W. A. (2005). *The sociology of childhood* (2nd ed.). Thousand Oaks, CA: Pine Forge Press.

Cox, S. (2005). Intention and meaning in young children's drawing. *Journal of Art and Design Education, 24*(2), 115–125.

Crotty, M. (1998). *The foundations of social research: Meaning and perspective in the research process.* Thousand Oaks, CA: Sage.

Darbyshire, P., MacDougall, C., & Schiller, W. (2005). Multiple methods in qualitative research with children: More insight or just more? *Qualitative Research, 5*(4), 417–436.

David, M., Edwards, R., & Alldred, P. (2001). Children and school-based research: "Informed consent" or "educated consent"? *British Educational Research Journal, 27*(3), 347–365.

Davidson, A. L. (1996). *Making and molding identity in schools: Student narratives on race, gender, and academic engagement.* Albany, NY: State University of New York Press.

Davies, B. (1982). *Life in the classroom and playground: The accounts of primary school children.* Boston: Routledge & Kegan Paul.

Davis, J. M. (1998). Understanding the meanings of children: A reflexive process. *Children and Society, 12*(5), 325–335.

Delgado, M. (2006). *Designs and methods for youth-led research.* Thousand Oaks, CA: Sage.

Dell Clark, C. (1999). The auto-driven interview: A photographic view-finder into children's experience. *Visual Sociology, 14,* 39–50.

Dempsey, J. V., & Tucker, S. A. (1994). Using photo-interviewing as a tool for research and evaluation. *Educational Technology, 34*(4), 55–62.

Denzin, N. K. (1977). *Childhood socialization: Studies in the development of language, social behavior, and identity.* San Francisco, CA: Jossey-Bass.

Denzin, N. K. (2001). The reflexive interview and a performative social science. *Qualitative Research, 1*(1), 23–46.

Dewey, J. (1980). *Art as experience.* New York: Perigee Books. (Original work published 1934)

Diamond, K. E. (1996). Preschool children's conceptions of disabilities: The salience of disability in children's ideas about others. *Topics in Early Childhood Special Education, 16*(4), 458–475.

Dockett, S., & Perry, B. (2003). Children's views and children's voices in starting school. *Australian Journal of Early Childhood, 28*(1), 12–17.

Douglas, K. B. (1998). Impressions: African American first-year students' perceptions of a predominantly white university. *Journal of Negro Education, 67*(4), 416–431.

Duff, W. (1975). *Images, stone, B.C.: Thirty centuries of northwest coast Indian sculpture.* Saanichton, British Columbia: Hancock House.

Edelsky, C., Searfoss, L. W., & Mersereau, Y. M. (1986). Variation and authenticity in a study of children's written humor. *Written Communication, 3,* 344.

Eder, D., & Corsaro, W. (1999). Ethnographic studies of children and youth: Theoretical and ethical issues. *Journal of Contemporary Ethnography, 28*(5), 520.

Eder, D., & Fingerson, L. (2003). Interviewing children and adolescents. In J. A. Holstein & J. F. Gubrium (Eds.), *Inside interviewing: New lenses, new concerns* (pp. 33–53). Thousand Oaks, CA: Sage.

Elbow, P. (1985). The shifting relationships between speech and writing. *College Composition and Communication, 36*(3), 283–303.

Epstein, D. (1998). Are you a girl or are you a teacher? The "least adult" role in research about gender and sexuality in a primary school. In G. Walford (Ed.), *Doing research about education* (pp. vii, 208). Bristol, PA: Falmer Press.

Evans, W. (1988). *American photographs.* New York: Museum of Modern Art. (Original work published 1938)

182 References

Evans-Winters, V. E. (2005). *Teaching black girls: Resiliency in urban classrooms*. New York: Peter Lang.

Farrell, T. J. (1978). Differentiating writing from talking. *College Composition and Communication, 29*(4), 346–350.

Fine, G. A., & Sandstrom, K. L. (1988). *Knowing children: Participant observation with minors*. Newbury Park, CA: Sage.

Fingerson, L. (2006). *Girls in power: Gender, body, and menstruation in adolescence*. Albany: State University of New York Press.

Fisher, D. D. V. (1991). *An introduction to constructivism for social workers*. New York: Praeger.

Foster, S., Hoge, J. D., & Rosch, R. H. (1999). Thinking aloud about history: Children's and adolescents' responses to historical photographs. *Theory and Research in Social Education, 27*(2), 179–214.

Fraser, S. (2004). Situating empirical research. In S. Fraser, V. Lewis, S. Ding, M. Kellett, & C. Robinson (Eds.), *Doing research with children and young people* (pp. 15–26). London: Sage.

Fraser, S., Lewis, V., Ding, S., Kellett, M., & Robinson, C. (2004). *Doing research with children and young people*. London: Sage.

Gaunt, K. D. (2006). *The games black girls play: Learning the ropes from Double Dutch to hip-hop*. New York: New York University Press.

Gauntlett, D. (2005). Using creative visual research methods to understand media audiences. *MedienPädagogik*. Retrieved July 6, 2006, from *www.medienpaed.com/04-1/gauntlett04-1.pdf*.

Gavin, M. (2003). Developing positive negatives: Youth on the edge capture images of their lives with help from PhotoVoice. *Children, Youth and Environments, 13*. Retrieved July 6, 2006, from *www.colorado.edu/journals/cye/13_2/FieldReports/PhotoVoice.htm*.

Gergen, K. J. (1999). *An invitation to social construction*. Thousand Oaks, CA: Sage.

Glauser, B. (1990). Street children: Deconstructing a construct. In A. James & A. Prout (Eds.), *Constructing and reconstructing childhood: Contemporary issues in the sociological study of childhood* (pp. 138–156). London: Falmer Press.

Goodwin, M. H. (2006). *The hidden life of girls: Games of stance, status, and exclusion*. Malden, MA: Blackwell.

Graue, M. E., & Walsh, D. J. (1998). *Studying children in context: Theories, methods, and ethics*. Thousand Oaks, CA: Sage.

Gray, M. L. (2004). *Coming of age in a digital era: Youth queering technologies in the rural United States*. PhD thesis in communication, University of California, San Diego.

Greene, S., & Hill, M. (2005). Researching children's experience: Methods and methodological issues. In S. Greene & D. Hogan (Eds.), *Researching children's experience: Approaches and methods* (pp. 1–19). London: Sage.

Haggerty, K. D. (2004). Ethics creep: Governing social science research in the name of ethics. *Qualitative Sociology, 27*(4), 391–414.

Halldén, G. (2003). Children's views of family, home and house. In P. Christensen & M. O'Brien (Eds.), *Children in the city: Home, neighborhood and community* (pp. 29–45). New York: Routledge.

Halpern, J. W. (1982). Review. *College Composition and Communication, 33*(4), 464–466.

Hardman, C. (1973). Can there be an anthropology of children? *Journal of the Anthropology Society of Oxford, 4*(1), 85–99.

Harper, D. (2002). Talking about pictures: A case for photo elicitation. *Visual Studies, 17*(1), 13–26.

Heisley, D. D., & Levy, S. J. (1991). Autodriving: A photoelicitation technique. *Journal of Consumer Research, 18,* 257–272.

Hennessy, E., & Heary, C. (2005). Exploring children's views through focus groups. In S. Greene & D. Hogan (Eds.), *Researching children's experience: Approaches and methods* (pp. 236–252). London: Sage.

Hessler, R. M., Downing, J., Beltz, C., Pelliccio, A., Powell, M., & Vale, W. (2003). Qualitative research on adolescent risk using e-mail: A methodological assessment. *Qualitative Sociology, 26*(1), 111–124.

Hogan, D. (2005). Researching "the child" in developmental psychology. In S. Greene & D. Hogan (Eds.), *Researching children's experiences: Approaches and methods* (pp. 22–41). London: Sage.

Holloway, S. L., & Valentine, G. (2000). Spatiality and the new social studies of childhood. *Sociology, 34*(4), 763–783.

Holmes, R. M. (1998). *Fieldwork with children.* Thousand Oaks, CA: Sage.

Holstein, J. A., & Gubrium, J. F. (1995). *The active interview.* Thousand Oaks, CA: Sage.

Holt, L. (2004). The "voices" of children: De-centering empowering research relations. *Children's Geographies, 2*(1), 13–27.

Hood, S., Kelley, P., & Mayall, B. (1996). Children as research subjects: A risky enterprise. *Children and Society, 10*(2), 117–128.

Hume, C., Salmon, J., & Ball, K. (2005). Children's perceptions of their home and neighborhood environments, and their association with objectively measured physical activity: A qualitative and quantitative study. *Health Education Research, 20*(1), 1–13.

Hurworth, R. (2003). Photo-interviewing for research. *Social Research Update, 40.* Retrieved December 30, 2003, from *sru.soc.surrey.ac.uk/ SRU40.html.*

Hurworth, R., Clark, E., Martin, J., & Thomsen, S. (2005). The use of photo-interviewing: Three examples from health evaluation and research. *Evaluation Journal of Australasia, 4*(1&2), 52–62.

James, A. (2001). Ethnography in the study of children and childhood. In P. Atkinson, A. Coffey, S. Delamont, J. Lofland, & L. Lofland (Eds.), *Handbook of ethnography* (pp. 246–257). Thousand Oaks, CA: Sage.

James, A., Jenks, C., & Prout, A. (1998). *Theorizing childhood.* New York: Teachers College Press.

James, A., & Prout, A. (1990). *Constructing and reconstructing childhood: New directions in the sociological study of childhood.* New York: Falmer Press.

James, A., & Prout, A. (1997). *Constructing and reconstructing childhood: Contemporary issues in the sociological study of childhood.* London: Falmer Press.

Jones, A. (2004). Involving children and young people as researchers. In S. Fraser, V. Lewis, S. Ding, M. Kellett, & C. Robinson (Eds.), *Doing research with children and young people* (pp. 113–130). Thousand Oaks, CA: Sage.

Jones, J. H. (1993). *Bad blood: The Tuskegee syphilis experiment.* New York: Free Press.

Jones, K. R., & Perkins, D. F. (2002). *Youth–adult partnerships.* University Park: Pennsylvania State University.

Kellett, M., Forrest, R., Dent, N., & Ward, S. (2004). "Just teach us the skills please, we'll do the rest": Empowering ten-year-olds as active researchers. *Children and Society, 18,* 329–343.

Kellett, M., Robinson, C., & Burr, R. (2004). Images of childhood. In S. Fraser, V. Lewis, S. Ding, M. Kellett, & C. Robinson (Eds.), *Doing research with children and young people* (pp. 27–42). Thousand Oaks, CA: Sage.

Kellogg, R. (1970). *Analyzing children's art.* Palo Alto, CA: National Press Books.

Kendrick, M., & McKay, R. (2004). Drawings as an alternative way of understanding young children's construction of literacy. *Journal of Early Childhood Literacy, 4*(1), 109–128.

Kitzinger, J., & Barbour, R. S. (1999). Introduction: The challenge and promise of focus groups. In R. S. Barbour & J. Kitzinger (Ed.), *Developing focus group research: Politics, theory and practice* (pp. 1–20). London: Sage.

Lansdown, G. (1994). Children's rights. In B. Mayall (Ed.), *Children's childhoods: Observed and experienced* (pp. 33–44). London: Falmer Press.

Lewis, A. (1992). Group child interviews as a research tool. *British Educational Research Journal, 18*(4), 413–421.

Lincoln, Y. S. (2005). Institutional review boards and methodological conservatism: The challenge to and from phenomenological paradigms. In N. K. Denzin & Y. S. Lincoln (Eds.), *The Sage handbook of qualitative research* (3rd ed., pp. 165–181). Thousand Oaks, CA: Sage.

Lindsay, G. (2000). Researching children's perspectives: Ethical issues. In A. Lewis & G. Lindsay (Eds.), *Researching children's perspectives* (pp. 3–20). Philadelphia: Open University Press.

Lortie, D. C. (1975). *School-teacher: A sociological study* (new preface 2002 ed.). Chicago: University of Chicago Press.

Lowenfeld, V. (1947). *Creative and mental growth.* New York: Macmillan.

Mandell, N. (1991a). The least-adult role in studying children. In F. C. Waksler (Ed.), *Studying the social worlds of children: Sociological readings* (pp. 38–59). London: Falmer Press.

Mandell, N. (1991b). Children's negotiation of meaning. In F. C. Waksler (Ed.), *Studying the social worlds of children: Sociological readings* (pp. 161–178). London: Falmer Press.

Markham, A. (1998). *Life online.* Walnut Creek, CA: Altamira Press.

Mason, J. S. (2000). Ethnography in cyberspace: Data collection via email and instant messaging. *Inkshed, 18*(1). Retrieved August 2, 2007, from *www.stthomasu.ca/inkshed/may00.htm.*

Mason, J. S. (2002). *From Gutenberg's galaxy to cyberspace: The transforming power of electronic hypertext.* Toronto: CITD Press, University of Toronto at Scarborough. Retrieved August 2, 2007, from *tspace.library.utoronto.ca/handle/1807/246.*

Mathison, S. (1988). Why triangulate? *Educational Researcher, 17*(2), 13–17.

Mathison, S. (2008). Seeing is believing: The credibility of image based research and evaluation. In S. Donaldson & C. Christie (Eds.), *The credibility of evidence.* Thousand Oaks, CA: Sage.

Mauthner, M. (1997). Methodological aspects of collecting data from children: Lessons from three research projects. *Children and Society*, *11*, 16–28.

Mayall, B. (1994). *Children's childhoods: Observed and experienced*. London: Falmer Press.

Mayall, B. (1996). *Children, health and the social order*. London: Open University Press.

Mayall, B. (2000). Conversations with children: Working with generational issues. In P. C. A. James (Ed.), *Research with children: Perspectives and practices* (pp. 120–135). London: Falmer Press.

Mayall, B., Bendelow, G., Storey, P., & Veltman, M. (1996). *Children's health in primary schools*. London: Falmer Press.

McDowell, L. (2001). "It's that Linda again": Ethical, practical, and political issues in longitudinal research with young men. *Ethics, Place and Environment*, *4*(2), 87–100.

McNiff, K. K. (1981). *Sex differences in children's art*. Unpublished doctoral dissertation, Boston University.

Mead, M., & Bateson, G. (1942). *Balinese character: A photographic analysis*. New York: New York Academy of Sciences.

Merleau-Ponty, M. (1962). *Phenomenology of perception* (C. Smith, Trans.). New York: Humanities Press.

Michell, L. (1999). Combining focus groups and interviews: Telling how it is; telling how it feels. In R. S. Barbour & J. Kitzinger (Ed.), *Developing focus group research: Politics, theory and practice* (pp. 36–46). London: Sage.

Morgan, D., Pacheco, V., Rodriguez, C., Vazquez, E., Berg, M., & Schensul, J. (2004). Youth participatory action research on hustling and its consequences: A report from the field. *Children, Youth and Environments*, *14*(2), 201–228. Retrieved August 9, 2007, from *www.colorado.edu/journals/cye/14_2/field4.pdf*.

Morgan, D. L. (1997). *Focus groups as qualitative research* (2nd ed.). Newbury Park, CA: Sage.

Morgan, M., Gibbs, S., Maxwell, K., & Britten, N. (2002). Hearing children's voices: Methodological issues in conducting focus groups with children aged 7–11 years. *Qualitative Research*, *2*(1), 5–20.

Morris-Roberts, K. (2001). Intervening in friendship exclusion? The politics of doing feminist research with teenage girls. *Ethics, Place and Environment*, *4*(2), 147–153.

Morrow, V. (2001). Using qualitative methods to elicit young people's perspectives on their environments: Some ideas for community health initiatives. *Health Education Research*, *16*(3), 255–268.

Morrow, V. (2003). "No ball games": Children's views of their urban environments. *Journal of Epidemiology and Community Health, 57*(4), 234.

Morrow, V., & Richards, M. (1996). The ethics of social research with children: An overview. *Children and Society, 10*(2), 90–105.

Morss, J. (1996). *Growing critical: Alternatives to developmental psychology.* London: Routledge.

Nespor, J. (1998). The meanings of research: Kids as subjects and kids as inquirers. *Qualitative Inquiry, 4*(3), 369–388.

Nespor, J. (2000). Anonymity and place in qualitative inquiry. *Qualitative Inquiry, 6,* 546–570.

Nieuwenhuys, O. (1994). *Children's lifeworlds: Gender, welfare and labour in the developing world.* London: Routledge.

Nunberg, G. (1990). *The linguistics of punctuation.* Chicago: University of Chicago Press.

Nuremberg Military Tribunals. (1949). *Trials of war criminals before the Nuremberg military tribunals under Control Council Law No. 10* (Vol. 2). Washington, DC: U.S. Government Printing Office.

Oldfather, P. (1995). Songs "come back to most of them": Students' experiences as researchers. *Theory into Practice, 34*(2), 131–137.

Oldfather, P., & Dahl, K. (1994). Toward a social constructivist reconceptualization of intrinsic motivation for literacy learning. *Journal of Reading Behavior, 26*(2), 139–153.

Opie, I., & Opie, P. (2000). *The lore and language of schoolchildren.* New York: New York Review Books Classics. (Original work published 1959)

Orenstein, P. (1994). *School girls: Young women, self-esteem, and the confidence gap.* New York: Doubleday.

Parker, W. C. (1984). Interviewing children: Problems and promise. *The Journal of Negro Education, 53*(1), 18–28.

Patton, M. Q. (2002). *Qualitative research & evaluation methods* (3rd ed.). Thousand Oaks, CA: Sage.

Pole, C. (2007). Researching children and fashion: An embodied ethnography. *Childhood, 14*(1), 67–84.

Prosser, J. (1998). *Image-based research: A sourcebook for qualitative researchers.* Philadelphia: Routledge/Falmer.

Punch, S. (2002a). Interviewing strategies with young people: The "secret box," stimulus material and task-based activities. *Children and Society, 16,* 45–56.

Punch, S. (2002b). Research with children: The same or different from research with adults? *Childhood, 9*(3), 321–341.

Punch, S. (2003). Childhoods in the majority world: Miniature adult or tribal child? *Sociology, 37*(2), 277–295.

Qvortrup, J. (1990). A voice for children in statistical and social accounting: A plea for children's rights to be heard. In A. James & A. Prout (Eds.), *Constructing and deconstructing childhood: Contemporary issues in the sociological study of childhood* (pp. 78–98). New York: Falmer Press.

Qvortrup, J. (1994). Introduction. In J. Qvortrup, M. Bardy, G. Sgritta, & H. Wintersberger (Eds.), *Childhood matters: Social theory, practice and politics* (pp. 1–23). Aldershot, UK: Avebury.

Reynolds, P. (1991). *Dance Civet Cat: Tonga children and labour in the Zambezi Valley.* Athens: Ohio University Press.

Roberts, H. (2000). Listening to children, and hearing them. In P. Christensen & A. James (Eds.), *Research with children: Perspectives and practice* (pp. 225–240). London: Falmer Press.

Rogers, A. G., Casey, M., Ekert, J., & Holland, J. (2005). Interviewing children using an interpretive poetics. In S. Greene & D. Hogan (Eds.), *Researching children's experience: Approaches and methods* (pp. 158–174). London: Sage.

Rose, G. (2001). *Visual methodologies: An introduction to the interpretation of visual materials.* Thousand Oaks, CA: Sage.

Rymes, B. (2001). *Conversational borderlands: Language and identity in an alternative urban high school.* New York: Teachers College Press.

Sabo, K. (Ed.). (2003). *Youth participatory evaluation: A field in the making.* San Francisco, CA: Jossey-Bass.

Schratz, M., & Walker, R. (1995). *Research as social change: New opportunities for qualitative research.* New York: Routledge.

Sieber, J. E. (2004). Empirical research on research ethics. *Ethics and Behavior, 14*(4), 397–412.

Silver, R. A. (2001). *Art as language: Access to emotions and cognitive skills through drawings.* London: Taylor & Francis.

Simmons, R. (2002). *Odd girl out: The hidden culture of aggression in girls.* New York: Harcourt.

Sinclair, R. (2004). Participation in practice: Making it meaningful, effective and sustainable. *Children and Society, 18,* 106–118.

Smith, F., & Barker, J. (2002). Contested spaces. *Childhood, 7*(3), 315–333.

Smith, L. T. (2005). On tricky ground: Researching the native in the age of uncertainty. In N. K. Denzin & Y. S. Lincoln (Eds.), *The*

Sage handbook of qualitative research (3rd ed., pp. 85–107). Thousand Oaks, CA: Sage.

Tammivaara, J., & Enright, S. D. (1986). On eliciting information: Dialogues with child informants. *Anthropology & Education Quarterly, 17*(4), 218–238.

Thomas, N., & O'Kane, C. (1998). The ethics of participatory research with children. *Children and Society, 12,* 336–348.

Thompson, R. A. (1992). Developmental changes in research and risk benefit: A changing calculus of concern. In B. Stanley & J. Sieber (Eds.), *Social research on children and adolescents: Ethical issues* (pp. 31–64). London: Sage.

Thorne, B. (1993). *Gender play: Girls and boys in school.* New Brunswick, NJ: Rutgers University Press.

Tisdall, E. K. M., & Davis, J. (2004). Making a difference? Bringing children's and young people's views into policy-making. *Children and Society, 18,* 131–142.

Trachtenberg, A. (1989). *Reading American photographs: Images as history, Mathew Brady to Walker Evans.* New York: Hill and Wang.

Van Manen, M. (1990). *Researching lived experience: Human science for an action sensitive pedagogy.* Albany: State University of New York Press.

Veale, A. (2005). Creative methodologies in participatory research with children. In S. Greene & D. Hogan (Eds.), *Researching children's experience: Approaches and methods* (pp. 253–272). London: Sage.

Wagener, D. K., Sporer, A. K., Simmerling, M., Flome, J. L., An, C., & Curry, S. J. (2004). Human participants challenges in youth-focused research: Perspectives and practices of IRB administrators. *Ethics and Behavior, 14*(4), 335–349.

Waksler, F. C. (1991). Studying children: Phenomenological insights. In F. C. Waksler (Ed.), *Studying the social world of children: Sociological readings* (pp. 60–69). New York: Falmer Press.

Wang, C. C., & Burris, M. A. (1994). Empowerment through photo novella: Portraits of participation. *Health Education Quarterly, 21*(2), 171–186.

Wang, C. C., & Burris, M. A. (1997). PhotoVoice: Concept, methodology and use for participatory needs assessment. *Health and Behaviour, 24*(3), 369–387.

Weber, S., & Mitchell, C. (2000). *That's funny, you don't look like a teacher: Interrogating images and identity in popular culture.* London: Falmer Press.

Weinger, S. (1998). Children living in poverty: Their perception of career opportunities. *Families in Society: The Journal of Contemporary Social Services, 79*, 320–330.

Westcott, H. L., & Davies, G. M. (1996). Sexually abused children's and young people's perspectives on investigative interviews. *British Journal of Social Work, 26*(4), 451–474.

Westcott, H. L., & Littleton, K. S. (2005). Exploring meaning in interviews with children. In S. Greene & D. Hogan (Eds.), *Researching children's experience: Approaches and methods* (pp. 141–157). London: Sage.

Wheatley, G. H. (1991). Constructivist perspectives on science and mathematics learning. *Science Education, 75*(1), 9–22.

Wheelock, A., Babell, D. J., & Haney, W. (2000). What can students' drawings tell us about high-stakes testing in Massachusetts? *Teachers College Record.* Retrieved February 5, 2001, from *www.tcrecord.org/ Content.asp?ContentID=10634.*

Winnicott, D. W. (1971). *Therapeutic consultations in child psychiatry.* New York: Basic Books.

Wolcott, H. F. (1994). *Transforming qualitative data: Description, analysis, and interpretation.* Thousand Oaks, CA: Sage.

Wortham, S. (2006). *Learning identity: The joint emergence of social identification and academic learning.* New York: Cambridge University Press.

Yuen, F. C. (2004). "It was fun . . . I liked drawing my thoughts": Using drawings as a part of the focus group process with children. *Journal of Leisure Research, 36.*

Zeiher, H. (2003). Shaping daily life in urban environments. In P. Christensen & M. O'Brien (Eds.), *Children in the city: Home, neighborhood and community* (pp. 66–81). New York: Routledge.

Index

About the Authors

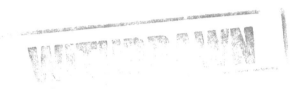

Melissa Freeman, PhD, is Assistant Professor of Qualitative Research Methodologies in the College of Education at the University of Georgia. Her research focuses on critical, constructivist, and relational approaches to educational research and evaluation; the role of dialogue in the construction of meaning and understanding; and the use of alternative elicitation strategies in interviewing and focus groups. She has worked with parents and young people in a variety of educational and youth services settings. Dr. Freeman's most recent research focuses on parents' and students' perceptions of accountability and testing in public schools.

Sandra Mathison, PhD, is Professor of Education at the University of British Columbia. Her research is in educational evaluation, and her work has focused especially on the potential and limits of evaluation to support democratic ideals and promote justice. She has conducted national large-scale and local evaluations of K–12, postsecondary, and informal educational programs and curricula. Dr. Mathison's most recent research focuses on the effects of state-mandated testing on teaching and learning, especially the impact on the work life of teachers and the educational experiences of students. She is editor of the *Encyclopedia of Evaluation,* coeditor (with E. Wayne Ross) of *Defending Public Schools: The Nature and Limits of Standards-Based Reform and Assessment* and *Battleground: Schools,* and Editor-in-Chief of the journal *New Directions for Evaluation.* She can be found on the web at *web.mac.com/sandra.mathison.*